# A Search for Truth

*"I Rest My Case"*

My Journey to Being Unchurched

ALEX VERCELLINO

PAGE PUBLISHING
Conneaut Lake, PA

First originally published by Page Publishing 2024

ISBN 979-8-89315-249-4 (pbk)
ISBN 979-8-89315-251-7 (digital)

Printed in the United States of America

# Contents

# *Preface*

They say we all have a book within us waiting to be written. This is the book I was meant to write. I've devoted most of my life thinking about this topic. I know there are a great many people with expert credentials who know a great deal more than I claim to know. That doesn't intimidate me since I believe everyone has to find their own way when it comes to their truth about God and religion. It's a personal journey.

If you have all the answers and don't like being challenged about your religious beliefs, you probably won't like this book. I know some people may be offended about what I've written. That isn't my intention. If that happens, I apologize. I hope enough people will see it as a sincere, thoughtful, and honest account of my personal search for truth about Christianity. I tried to be as accurate as I could when referring to historical events. At the same time, I don't expect everyone to agree with all my speculations, opinions, or conclusions. We all see the world through our own personal filters and often see the same things differently. I respect the fact that others might hold different views. My hope is that what I've written will serve to stimulate thought and dialogue. While I plead guilty of demonizing Christianity, it wasn't my intention. I wrote it for the following reasons:

1.  To encourage dialogue about God and religion
2.  To share ideas and information about Christianity most people won't learn in church
3.  To help people who don't embrace Christianity understand why they might have made that decision and why they should feel okay with it
4.  To encourage more moderation among believers.

Some may argue my book isn't fair and balanced. I plead guilty. I didn't think there was a need for another book extolling the virtues of Christianity. There are thousands of books like that overflowing the shelves in libraries and bookstores. I felt there was a greater need for a book that presents a different view than what people usually learn when they read about Christianity or attend a Christian Church. My book is about a search for truth.

There are other nonbeliever books on the market. Most of them are written to promote atheism. My book is different. It's less about God and more about religion. The concept of God refers to the profound question about whether a creator exists, along with the claim that he's the source of everything that's known and unknown. The existence of such a creator can't be proved or disproved and is a topic onto itself. That's not what this book is about. It's about what I learned about Christianity. Christianity doesn't question the existence of a creator. It goes so far as to describe him with having characteristics with humanlike strengths and flaws. I concluded Christianity is the creation of man and not God. It comes in many forms, containing a multitude of different beliefs about what it means to be a Christian. I challenge many of those beliefs and point out where they have taken us to dark places time has made us regret.

I hope what I've written will help make Christianity a better force for good in the world. There's nothing wrong with a little self-criticism and introspection. That's something many people in the Christian community have difficulty doing. It's my hope that even if people continue to cling to their Christian faith after reading this book, they'll be more informed and thoughtful.

This book is most critical of fundamental Christians and the Christian right. While it might be a small segment of the Christian family, their voices are often so loud they appear to speak for all Christians and sometimes for our country. My quarrel with mainstream Christianity is that it hasn't challenged fundamental Christians when they misrepresent what they believe to be true or morally right.

# The Search

*What I came to understand about what was important was not
so much what we believed but how we choose to live our lives. I'm
comfortable letting the concept of God become the better angels
within us rather than the mythical God from ancient times. I think
eternity will take care of itself since I believe we're all one human
family and share the same fate regardless of what we believe.*

—Al Vercellino

I've been curious about spirituality and religion since I was a young child. My parents were nonpracticing Catholics. We seldom went to church. I knew very little about religion. Few of my friends attended church. Most people in my situation would have probably attended a few churches that were similar to their family or friend's church. In time, they would have found a place of worship where they would be comfortable and could achieve spiritual satisfaction. Had I done that I would have probably joined the Catholic Church, but I wasn't ready to embrace any religion. I was more interested in seeking answers to questions about God and the meaning of life. My search encompassed all the major religions. I was driven more by curiosity and a search for the truth rather than accepting faith-based answers.

I remember even as a young child being fascinated with televangelists like Oral Roberts, Billy Graham, and later Jim and Tammy Baker, Pat Robertson, Benny Hinn, and Joel Osteen. If anything, they made a skeptic out of me in addition to raising my curiosity about their followers. They inspired me to want to learn more about religion and people of faith. It became a lifelong pursuit.

Early on I discovered all the major religions embraced similar core beliefs about how people should live their lives and treat one another. At the time, I thought they all promoted a way of life that brought out the best in everyone. I soon learned that wasn't necessarily true. I learned about their ancient texts that described people and events that required faith in order to be a believer and made claims about chosen people in ancient times who got their information directly from God, like Moses, Jesus, Mohammad, and more recently Joseph Smith of the Latter-day Saints. Their ancient texts were not without some historical value, but their claims of being based on the Word of God couldn't be proved using historical or scientific evidence. It became clear to me that to accept one ancient text as true meant the others weren't true. They couldn't all be right.

I learned about the evolution of religions and how they evolved. When people needed explanations about events they couldn't control or understand, they turned to God to answer those questions—like what controlled the weather, abundance, famine, what system of morality was needed to promote the stability of the social unit, and what happens when we die. What people didn't understand they attributed to God or gods. Separate religions developed throughout the world to give answers to those questions. They were first passed down from one generation to another by word of mouth and then in written form. Early religions consisted of many gods (polytheism) and eventually evolved into religions consisting of only one god (monotheism). The origins of almost all religious beliefs can be traced to earlier religions or to other religions of their time. Beliefs didn't arise in a vacuum. Their roots could be traced. For example, Christianity and Islam have their roots in the God of Abraham (Judaism), and they all have their roots in Zoroastrianism.

The religion of Zoroastrianism was founded in Persia between 1500 and 1000 bc. Its theology influenced Judaism, Christianity, and Islam. It gave birth to the concepts of God, Satan, the soul, heaven and hell, savior, resurrection, and final judgment. Knowing where those concepts originated took away their mysticism. It also planted the seed in me that all religions were the creation of man and not God.

In my study of the major religions, I learned that Jains and Buddhists were the most tolerant. Christians and Muslims were the least tolerant since they both share the common characteristic of being proselytizing faiths and have a long history of committing harm to others who don't share in their beliefs. To accept Christianity, Islam, or Judaism required that I accept their founders who were described in ancient texts as receiving their information directly from God. To accept Buddhism and Hinduism required that I accept reincarnation. If I had to pick a major religion that promoted the most "godlike" practices and had the best history of living in harmony with the rest of the world, it would have been Buddhism. Based on what I had learned, I couldn't embrace any of the religions based on their claim of knowing the absolute truth.

I also came to understand the moral beliefs of religions are not all that profound. For example, thou shall not kill, steal, lie, cheat, rob, or rape. Thou shall do unto others as you would like done onto you, be faithful to your spouse, love your children, respect your parents, and be honest in your relations with others. There's nothing mystical about any of those beliefs. They didn't need to come from God on a stone tablet to become the bedrock of moral beliefs needed for the long-term survival of social units or civilized society. Ironically, there's no indication that religious people observe those moral beliefs any better than people who are not religious. Christopher Hitchens, the author of *God is Not Great: How Religion Poisons Everything*, has said many times, "No one has ever been able to give me one moral belief that Christians hold to be true that couldn't also be held true by a nonbeliever. The only exclusive claim made by organized religions is what happens after we die, and that's where they offer a market basket of choices."

I've always been puzzled about why Christians believe what ancient people said about God between two thousand and three thousand years ago when most everything they knew in those days turned out to be wrong? They believed the world was flat, knew nothing about the solar system or gravity, the human body, practiced poor hygiene, and thought it was morally okay to enslave others. Their ancient texts claimed the earth was created by God in six days and that Adam and Eve were the first humans to inhabit the earth; that Eve came from Adam's rib; that suffering and death came about because Adam and Eve ate the forbidden fruit; that a snake, donkey, and burning bush talked to people; that the world was flooded by an angry God and was saved by Noah, who built an ark 450 feet long, seventy-five feet wide, and forty-five feet high and filled it with one pair of all the animals that inhabited the earth; that Moses had a magic wand; that the Nile was turned into blood; that food rained from the sky for forty years; that fish and bread magically multiplied to feed the hungry; that the devil exists and is the cause of all evil in the world; that a fiery lake of eternal torment awaits unbelievers under the earth; that there are witches, wizards, and sorcerers; that Jesus brought the dead back to life, including himself, walked on water, turned water into wine, and long after his death forgives all our sins and provides salvation to those who believe in him. If these ancient stories in the Bible are unbelievable, then how do we decide what is believable?

I've always been critical of people who claim to have all the answers. When I ask how they know, they usually say it's what their family and church taught them. Their knowledge is often shallow, and they know little about the other great religions or that of non-believers. Outside of what they've been taught to believe, they have little or no curiosity.

All that I learned didn't leave me without some basis for living my life since all the major religions promoted many of the same basic messages about morality. Early in my search, I turned to a Buddhist saying, "From good comes good and from evil comes evil," which I decided would become the foundation for how I would live my life. While that statement seemed simple, I thought it profound. I didn't need an ancient text to help me decide good and evil or right from wrong. Any sane person has that capacity. The challenge is to practice good over evil. It's what the Hindus and Buddhists call good and bad karma. I felt this simple rule along with the golden rule placed me in harmony with the "good" in most of the religions even though it didn't answer the question about why we're here or what happens after we die, but then I didn't think any of the religions could prove they had answers to those questions. I concluded I could live without those answers.

If there is one universal moral rule in all the major religions, it would be the golden rule. It's the major thread of morality that connects all the major religions.

What I came to understand about what was important was not so much what we believed but how we choose to live our lives. I'm comfortable letting the concept of God become the better angels within us rather than the mythical God from ancient times. I think eternity will take care of itself since I believe we're all one human family and share the same fate regardless of what we believe.

I also learned I was not alone in my search and that even though the vast majority claim to believe in God, close to a third don't believe in the biblical God.* Thirty-five percent of Americans say they practice a blended form of religion while the fastest-growing group are people who don't subscribe to any religion.* Other industrialized countries show even lower church attendance than in the US. It appears most people are struggling with many of the questions I have about organized religions.

---

* "How Many People Go Regularly To Weekly Religious Services," Religious Tolerance. Org, Ontario Consultants on Religious Tolerance, n.d., http://www. religioustolerance.org/rel_rate.htm (March 21, 2005).

* *Time Almanac* (160 Gould Street, Needham, MA: Pearson Education, 2005) 358. People who don't subscribe to any religion are the fastest growing group in the United States.

# Christ and Christianity

*Historians did not record his birth. Nor for 30 years, did anyone
pay him much heed. A Jew from the Galilean hill country with a
reputation for teaching and healing, he showed up at the age of 33 in
Jerusalem during Passover. In three days, he was arrested, tried and
convicted of treason, then executed like the commonest of criminals.
His followers said that God raised him from the dead. Except among
those who believed in him, the event passed without notice.**

—*Newsweek*, March 29, 1999

Not having received religious instruction while growing up, I had
a lot of questions about Christ and Christianity, so I began reading
about Jesus and the Christian movement. Over time I found answers
to most of my questions.

There are two ways to look at the evolution of Christianity
and Christ—through faith and through history. I chose to look at
faith and apply it to what we know about the history of Christ and
Christianity. I also looked at how the evolution of Christianity was
changed by people and events. I couldn't help but speculate on how
Christianity might have evolved differently had people and events
been different.

"There is much we don't know about the life of Christ." Albert
Schweitzer said, "We all find the Jesus we want because we know so
little about him." Outside the Gospels, there's no historical record
documenting the life of Jesus. The historical documentation most

---

* Anne Underwood, "2000 Years of Jesus" (Newsweek, March 29,1999), 52. The
quote, "Historians did not record his birth…

Christians point to is from Josephus Flavius; however, most scholars believe his references to Jesus were forged and added sometime during the beginning of the fourth century.*

In my search, I found answers to the following questions:

**Where did the Gospels come from?** They were written by mortal men who were given the names of Matthew, Mark, Luke, and John. Contrary to popular belief, God was not the author. Earlier followers believed that Matthew and John may have been apostles of Christ and could have known him. They speculated that Mark was a follower of Peter, and Luke a follower of Paul, and neither was thought to have known Christ. Mark was the first gospel written, and many scholars believe Matthew and Luke used Mark in their writings along with an unknown source called *Q.* While each gospel is named, no one knows who actually wrote them. It's commonly accepted they were written at different times for different audiences and were not intended to be written as historical documents. They were written to promote Jesus. No original documents of the Gospels have ever been found, and there's been an ongoing debate about how some of the passages and words were translated. Other issues include the many discrepancies, contradictions, and omissions found within the four gospels.

Most scholars now believe Jesus's followers couldn't read or write and couldn't have been authors of the Gospels. It's believed they were written anonymously with none of the writers being an eyewitness to the events they wrote about.* Most scholars also believe they were written by highly educated, Greek-speaking Christians who probably lived somewhere outside of Palestine.*

---

* Dan Barker, *Losing Faith in Faith* (Freedom From Religion Foundation, Inc. PO Box 750, Madison, WI. 1992), 361–364. However, most scholars believe the references to Jesus that Christians refer to were forged and added sometimes during he beginning of the fourth century.

* Bart D. Ehrman, *Interrupted,* (New York, NY: HarperCollins, 2009), 103. Most scholars now believe Jesus's followers couldn't read or write and couldn't have been authors of the Gospels. It's believed they were written anonymously with none of the writers being an eyewitness to the events they wrote about.

* Ibid., 106. Most believe they were written by highly educated, Greek speaking Christians who probably lived somewhere outside of Palestine.

**When were the Gospels written?** When Jesus was alive, most scholars believe he was almost a complete unknown outside his small circle of followers. The first documented historical record of anything written about him was in AD 112.*

The reason why nothing was written until long after his death is because his followers thought he was going to return in the second coming of Christ and bring about the kingdom of God at any moment or at least during their lifetime. That didn't happen, so the apostles and the first-generation Christians concluded it was important to start preserving the sayings of Jesus and spreading the Gospels. Thus the beginning of the Jesus movement.

Scholars believe the four gospels were written sixty to 125 years after the death of Jesus. Some Christians argue the first gospels were written thirty years after his death. The exact number of years is not certain and is a matter of debate.

**Were there other early Christian groups?** During the early years of Christianity, there were a number of groups that held different beliefs about Jesus. The most notable among them were the Ebionites, Marcionists, and the Gnostics. The Ebionites believed, like Jesus's brother James, that he was fully human and not divine. The Marcionists believed like Paul that Jesus was fully divine. The Gnostic believed he was both divine and human and that salvation didn't come from having faith in Jesus's death and resurrection but by understanding the secret teachings he revealed. They were all thriving members of the Jesus movement in their respective regions and, like today's Christians, had written documents to support their beliefs.

They might have continued to flourish had it not been for the Roman Emperor Constantine, who saw a need to resolve the conflicts within the Christian community. He called together a group of Christian leaders in AD 325 to the First Ecumenical Council in Nicaea, where church leaders pulled together the various factions within the Jesus movement. It was there that Jesus the man was declared equal to God. During the Second Ecumenical Council in

---

* Ibid., 149. The first documented historical record of anything written about him was in AD 112.

AD 328, the Trinity was created, which is the concept of the Father, Son, and Holy Spirit. From that point on, other competing Christian sects were labeled heretical and eventually disappeared from the Christian landscape.

The twenty-seven books of the New Testament were never officially approved by a church council. They evolved over a three hundred-year period driven by numerous historical and cultural factors within the Christian movement. They were first put forth by Athanasius, the bishop of Alexandria, Egypt, in AD 367 and later became the de facto list that Christians have come to know as the New Testament.* Contrary to popular belief, they didn't come from divine intervention as many Christians believe but instead, evolved from the influence of mortal men over a three hundred-year period. The issue of what should be included is still not totally resolved. The Catholic Church, Eastern Orthodox, and some Protestants denominations still don't totally agree on what books to include.

Over time, the church discouraged any other inquiry about the life of Jesus. Thus, little attention was given to the gospels of Thomas, Peter, Philip, or Mary Magdalene, and others. At the same time, early Christians such as the Ebionites, Marcionites, Gnostics were relegated to the scrap heap of Christian history. Had the church allowed other Christian sects to flourish and other gospels to survive Christianity would have more than likely evolved differently than we know it today.

It took the church between 325 and 367 years to agree on what to believe about Jesus. That's a long time, knowing how the story evolved should raise serious doubts about the claims Christians make about him.

Some might say the Roman brand of Christianity won out because they got it right, and the others got it wrong. The Roman

---

* Ibid., 220–221. Contrary to popular belief the 27 books of the New Testament were never officially approved by a church council. They evolved over a three-hundred-year period driven by numerous historical and cultural factors within the Christian movement. They were first put forth by Athanasius, the bishop of Alexandria, Egypt in AD 367 and later became the defacto list that Christians have come to know as the New Testament.

brand prevailed because it became the official religion of the Roman Empire. Its hierarchical structure and military-like command and control also aided in its growth. It's interesting to note that after the fall of the Roman Empire when Christianity became a dominate force in the world civilization slipped into the period historians call the Dark Ages.

Today we still have the Catholic Church claiming they're still right, but since the Reformation, we now have thirty-four thousand Protestant denominations also claiming they're right.

**What brought about the growth of Christianity?** Until AD 313, Christians were persecuted. Had that continued, Christianity may have met the fate of many other ancient religions and could have been destined to obscurity. That didn't happen. The Roman Emperor Constantine gave Christians freedom to worship in AD 313. In the late fourth century, Christianity was made the official religion of Rome and, as a result, spread throughout the world. Before that, the Jesus movement belonged to the people and not the church.

After the fall of the Roman Empire, the monks became the safe keepers of the church and can be credited with preserving the written documents during the Dark Ages. There's also evidence they altered some of the documents. We can never underestimate man's fallibility and his ability to fabricate. There's every reason to believe some changes were made in the documents.

The Crusades (1095–1291) helped Christianity establish itself as a world power. That was followed by the Inquisition (1352 to the early nineteenth century), a five hundred-year period when the church dominated Western civilization. The Inquisition was characterized by threats of damnation, hell, and even punishment and death to anyone who didn't embrace the faith. The church sustained itself in part through threat and intimidation. Ironically, the same Jesus who preached peace and love was used to justify both those events.

The Protestant Reformation in the sixteenth century with Martin Luther (1483–1546) and John Calvin (1509–1564) changed the landscape of Christianity forever. The break from the Roman Catholic Church didn't come without a struggle, but it eventually prevailed and produced tens of thousands Christian denominations, all claiming to know best what it means to be a Christian.

The advent of the printing press in the 1500s added another significant change. The scriptures were no longer the expressed domain of the clergy. People could read the Gospels in their native language and interpret their meaning themselves or with the help of religious leaders of their choice. As a result, the Catholic Church's grip on the Jesus movement became greatly diminished.

**Since Jesus was a Jew, where did Christianity come from?** Christianity arose out of Judaism with his followers claiming Jesus fulfilled many of the promises in the Old Testament. Jesus never claimed to be a Christian. There were no Christians when he lived. The birth of Christianity as a new religion can be traced to Paul. He persecuted the first Christians until claiming to have experienced a vision of Christ on the road to Damascus. Three years later, he met Peter and James, the brother of Jesus. By asserting that non-Jewish disciples of Christ didn't have to observe Jewish law, he helped establish Christianity as a separate religion rather than a Jewish sect. It was because of Paul, more than anyone else, that Christianity became a world religion. Jesus's brother James and the other apostles didn't agree with Paul. It can be argued Paul hijacked the Christian movement from James and the original followers of Jesus. No serious biblical scholar would disagree that Jesus lived and died as a Jew and made no claim during his lifetime of founding a separate religion.

Had it not been for Paul who didn't know Jesus and whose ideas were not embraced by the other apostles, Christianity would have evolved much differently than we currently know it. Had Paul not been successful in promoting his point of view, the Christian faith would have continued to exist as a Jewish sect and its appeal would have been greatly reduced by both Jews and non-Jews. Most likely it wouldn't have evolved into a major religion.

There has never been anything that has come close to equaling what Paul achieved. He offered salvation to anyone who agreed to give up what they believed and accept his claim that Jesus died for their sins. That simple belief created institutions that generated unequaled power and wealth and shaped the world like no other idea in the history of mankind.

**What about Jesus being the Son of God?** In his book *The Jesus Dynasty*, James Tabor writes that Jesus believed he was the Davidic Messiah* and made no claim of being the Son of God. He attributes Paul, who never met Jesus, for planting that seed.* History shows it was Paul who dominated the movement after the death of Jesus and promoted the belief he was the Son of God and died for our sins. He influenced what the early church came to believe about the life of Jesus and his mission. It was not a belief held by his brother James and the original followers of Jesus. Tabor's evidence is compelling.

Three of the gospel writers don't refer to Jesus as divine. In none of the speeches in Acts is Jesus spoken as divine. For ancient Jews, being "the Son of God" didn't mean divine. In the Old Testament, it meant being the human intermediary for God on earth or the one God has chosen to do his will. John is the only gospel that identifies Jesus as divine.*

To add to the confusion, John links Christ with God at the very birth of the universe. Mark claims it happened with his baptism. Matthew and Luke say it was the Nativity. Paul claims it was on the day of his resurrection.*

Jews and Muslims acknowledge Jesus's existence but view him as a prophet and teacher and not God. There's no historical evidence

---

* James D. Tabor. *The Jesus Dynasty. The Hidden History of Jesus, His Royal Family, and the Birth of Christianity* (New York, NY: Simon & Schuster, 2006), 282. Jesus believed he was the Davidic Messiah.

* Ibid., 280. Made no claim of being the Son of God. He attributes Paul, who never met Jesus but claims to have seen him in a vision for planting that seed.

* Ehrman, 245–249. Three of the Gospels writers don't call Jesus God. In none of the speeches in Acts is Jesus spoken as divine. For ancient Jews being "the son of God" didn't mean divine. In the Old Testament it meant being the human intermediary for God on Earth or the one God has chosen to do his will. John, who was an advocate for Paul, is the only Gospel that identifies Jesus divine.

* Ibid., 94. John links Christ with God at the very birth of the universe. Mark claims it happened with his baptism. Matthew and Luke identify Christ with becoming the Son of God with the Nativity and Paul on the day of his resurrection.

to support the claim that he was divine. That's even a stretch when looking at the Gospels. We have to remember it took the church until AD 325 to officially arrive at that decision.

**What about Jesus being the Messiah?** During the time of Jesus, the Jews were being persecuted by the Romans and were looking for the Messiah to come and rescue them from their conquers. In Judaism, the Messiah is the expected king from the line of David who will deliver the Jews from foreign bondage and restore Israel to its golden age. There were others at about the time of Jesus who made that claim. It was something people expected to happen. The time was right for someone to be declared the Messiah, much like a self-fulling prophecy. As it turned out, Jesus never restored Israel to its golden age.

In order for Jesus to become the Messiah, the writers had to establish that he was a descendant of David. Those were ancient times when recordkeeping was almost nonexistent, yet the gospel writers attempted to make the connection. The fact is they probably made it up. Both Matthew and Luke describe different links. "Matthew traces Joseph's descendants from King David via twenty-eight intermediate generations while Luke has forty-one generations." To make matters worse, there is almost no overlap in the names on the two lists.* The apologists have an explanation for those differences, but to do so, they have to stretch rational thinking beyond its limits.

It was John the baptizer (Jesus's cousin) who first preached about the kingdom of God, and it was Jesus who joined him and his movement, thus becoming a disciple of John.* When John the baptizer was executed by Herod, Jesus was left to carry on the mission. He did that until his untimely death a year later. Upon Jesus's death, his brother James succeeded him as the leader of the movement. The

---

*  Richard Dawkins, *The God Delusion,* (Boston & New York: Houghton Mifflin Company, 2006), 95. "Matthew traces Joseph's descent from King David via twenty-eight intermediate generations, while Luke has forty-one generations." To make matters worse, there is almost no overlap in the names on the two lists.

*  Tabor, 135. In Tabor's quest for the historical Jesus he believes it was John the Baptizer (Jesus's cousin) who first preached about the Kingdom of God, and it was Jesus who joined him and his movement thus becoming a disciple of John.

early Christian Church in Rome downplayed James who was a Jew and deferred to Paul, who diminished the Jewishness of Jesus and welcomed gentiles into the new religion.

According to Tabor, John and Jesus believed they were living in the "last days" or the "end of the age"* and that "God would raise up a king of the line of David, who would be instrumental in throwing off foreign rule and establish an independent Kingdom of Israel, thus inaugurating the new age of peace and justice in the entire world."* He goes on to write, "The good news of the kingdom of God predicted the apocalyptic reversal of society from top to bottom. Those in power would fall, and those oppressed would be lifted."* Contrary to popular belief, they anticipated a kingdom on earth and not in heaven.* As we know now, Jesus didn't drive the Romans out or establish Israel as a sovereign state. Instead, he was crucified like the commonest of criminals with his death not even causing a ripple outside of his immediate family and a few of his close followers.

When it became clear Jesus was not going to return and bring with him the kingdom of God on earth, John, the last gospel writer, declared the kingdom of God would not be on earth but instead be in heaven, and that's what most Christians believe today.

**What about Paul?** Those who study the Christian movement would have to agree that James, the brother of Jesus, became the successor of Jesus and the undisputed leader of the Christian movement after his death.* James was next in line with the royal Davidic blood-

---

* Ibid., 157. They (John and Jesus) believed they were living in the "last days" or the "end of the age."

* 154–155. "God would raise up a King of the line of David who would be instrumental in throwing off foreign rule and establishing an independent Kingdom of Israel, thus inaugurating the New Age of peace and justice in the entire world."

* Ibid., 172. "The Good News of the Kingdom of God, predicted the apocalyptic reversal of society from top to bottom. Those in power would fall, and those oppressed would be lifted."

* Ibid., 280. Contrary to popular belief they anticipated a Kingdom on earth and not in heaven (p. 280).

* Ibid., 244. James, the brother of Jesus, became the successor of Jesus and the undisputed leader of the Christian movement after his death.

line. Yet as it turns out, the early Roman Church chose to accept Paul's version of Christ while dismissing James and the apostles chosen by Jesus who were left to carry on his mission.

Paul was a Roman citizen who saw himself as the "apostle to the Gentiles," viewing himself as the thirteenth apostle.* His writings appeared in the mid-'50s, before the other gospels were written. He de-emphasized the Jewishness of Jesus, insisting Gentile converts were not required to be circumcised or live as Jews under the Torah.* This kind of thinking was a departure from what Jesus believed and what James and the other apostles believed. Since Paul never claimed he knew Jesus when he was alive, he seldom mentions anything about his earthly life and what he said. Instead, he refers to a disembodied spiritual Christ speaking from the sky. He says nothing about his birth, doesn't mention anything about miracles, fixes no historical times or places to events surrounding his life, makes no references to the twelve apostles by name, omits the trial, and doesn't name the location and place of the crucifixion.*

It was Paul who set the stage for what the early church adopted as the core of Christ's message. That is "Christ as the divine, preexistent Son of God who took on human form, died on the cross for the sins of the world and was resurrected to heavenly glory at God's right hand…"* It was Paul who declared Jesus's purpose was to die on the cross as atonement for the sins of the world, and those who accept his atoning sacrifice will receive the gift of eternal life.*

---

* Ibid., 261. Paul was a Roman citizen who saw himself as the "Apostle to the Gentiles" viewing himself as the Thirteenth Apostle.
* Ibid., 267. He deemphasized the Jewishness of Jesus insisting Gentile converts were not required to be circumcised or live as Jews under the Torah.
* Barker, 368. He says nothing about miracles; fixes no historical times or places to events surrounding the life of Jesus; makes no references to the twelve apostles by name; omits the trial and doesn't name the location and place of the crucifixion.
* Tabor, 273. "Christ as the divine, preexistent Son of God who took on human form, died on the cross for the sins of the world, and was resurrected to heavenly glory at God's right hand…"
* Ibid., 264. It was Paul who declared Jesus' purpose was to die on the cross as atonement for the sins of the world and that those who accept his atoning

When the writings about Christ were canonized, Paul was given major press. He was named as the author of thirteen of the twenty-seven books of the New Testament. The book of Acts (written by Luke) is almost entirely a defense of Paul's revelations as the thirteenth apostle. Luke was a pro-Roman, a Gentile, and the only non-Jewish writer in the New Testament.* If everything that is attributed to Paul was taken from the scriptures, there would be little left of what we call Christianity. Yet Paul didn't know Christ when he was alive and attributes everything to his alleged vision. If someone were to make that claim today, they'd be labeled a charlatan or at worst, insane.

The early church said little about James and the other apostles selected by Jesus after his death. Had they accepted the message of James, the central message of Christianity would have been much different from what Christians believe today. It's not likely there would have been anything said about his virgin birth, the resurrection, or that he died on the cross to atone for our sins. "James directly disputed Paul's teaching of salvation by faith without the deeds of the law."* Most likely, James's central messages would have been about the Messiah and God ushering in the kingdom of God on earth and not heaven; the need to worship God (not Jesus); that sin is forgiven through repentance and prayer along with the moral and ethical teachings of Jesus. Jesus would have been regarded as a great teacher and prophet, much like what the Jews and Muslims believe about him.

We have to remember the Romans were the victors in their battles with the Jews and, as a result, claimed the right to decide how history would be written. When they decided to adopt Christianity, it's easy to understand why they chose to diminish the Jewishness of Christ and give the glory of this new religion to the Gentiles. They

---

sacrifice will receive the gift of eternal life.

* Ibid., 249. He's named as the author of 13 of the 27 books of the New Testament. The book of Acts (written by Luke) is almost entirely a defense of Paul's revelations as the thirteenth Apostle. Luke was a pro-Roman, a Gentile and the only non-Jewish writer in the New Testament.

* Tabor, 274. "James directly disputed Paul's teaching of salvation by faith without the deeds of the law."

conquered, ruled, and later persecuted Jews. Why would they want to make a Jew the central figure in their state-run religion? It's easy to see why the New Testament has the Roman version or Paul's account of Christ's life and mission. They even went so far as to diminish Rome's role in the death of Jesus and placed almost all of the blame on the Jews. Sadly, their claims were used to justify two thousand years of Jewish persecution, resulting in the longest period of genocide the world has ever known.

**What do the Gospels say about the birth of Christ?** Nowhere are the differences and inconsistencies in the scriptures more apparent than what the Gospels tell us about Jesus's birth. Only two of the four gospel writers say anything about his birth. That would be Matthew and Luke, and they both give different accounts of that event while writing to different audiences. Because of the inconsistencies, a literal interpretation of the scriptures would be impossible when trying to account for the story of his birth.

Matthew wrote a decade before Luke. He offered wise men, a star, and put baby Jesus in a house. Most scholars believe his account was directed toward Jews. Luke offered shepherds and a manger. Scholars believe his account was directed toward Gentiles. Both mention Bethlehem as the place of the virgin birth. Some say the destination to Bethlehem is a theological necessity since Bethlehem had been David's hometown. Both connect his birth with the Jewish prophecy in the Old Testament about the coming of the Messiah. There is no evidence of Jesus, Mary, or Joseph ever speaking of his birth. Scholars believe the story of his life did not begin with his birth but with the passion and resurrection since that was the defining moment of his life and the Christian movement.

In Matthew's version of Mary's pregnancy, he said Joseph was first humiliated by the news his future wife was pregnant. Later in a dream, an unnamed angel brought news that what was conceived in her was of the Holy Ghost.

Matthew portrayed Mary and Joseph as residents of Bethlehem. He had them leaving for Egypt and eventually to Nazareth because Herod ordered the death of all local children under the age of two in order to kill the child he has learned will one day be king of the Jews.

Historians cannot validate this story about Herod. If it happened, it's hard to believe there's no mention of it outside the writings of Matthew. It would have been a huge event. Many believe the basis for Matthew's version was to draw a parallel with the Pharaoh's murder of all male infants of Israel in Exodus.

Matthew mentioned wise men from the east, guided by a star, who went in search of the baby Jesus. The use of stars marking historical events was common in those days. Stars were associated with the founding of Rome and the fall of Jerusalem, along with the birth of Alexander the Great and Augustus Caesar.*

Luke offered a different account. It's the one most Christians have come to embrace when celebrating his birth. In Luke's account, he said Mary found herself in the presence of the Angel Gabriel. He told Mary, "And behold, thou shalt conceive in thy womb, and bring forth a son, and shalt call his name Jesus. He shall be great, and shall be called the Son of the Highest." Luke is the only one who gives this account of Jesus's birth.

Luke doesn't mention a journey to Egypt, nor is it mentioned anywhere in the scriptures. In order for Luke to get Mary and Joseph to Bethlehem, he mentioned they were on a brief visit to Joseph's home to comply with the census. However, according to historical records, there was no call for a census at that time. A census did take place twelve years later.*

Other than Matthew and Luke, the claim of the virgin birth is found nowhere else in the New Testament. Some scholars believe the word virgin was originally meant to mean young girl and was misinterpreted when translated. Most scholars agree Joseph was not the father of Jesus and Mary was not married to Joseph at the time of his

---

* Broward Liston? Orlando, Amanda Bower/New York, Helen Gibson/London and Marguerite Michaels/Arlington Heights, *Behind the First Noel, (Time, December 13, 2004),* 53 58. The use of stars marking historical events were common in those days. Stars were associated with the founding of Rome and the fall of Jerusalem, along with the birth of Alexander the Great and Augustus Caesar.

* Ibid., 53. 51–52. Matthew and Luke's version of the Birth of Christ. A census did take place twelve years later.

birth. There are clues in the early writings about Jesus that suggest Mary had an affair. During Jesus's life, it was rumored the father was a Roman soldier named Panthera. There are also claims that after learning she was pregnant, Mary left town to stay with close family relatives (Elizabeth and Zechariah—the parents of John the baptizer who lived in Ein Kerem).* That would be normal behavior for someone who became pregnant out of wedlock. There are references in early writings about Jesus that suggests he was "born of fornication" and not divine intervention.*

Catholics and the Eastern Orthodox Church believe Mary remained a virgin during and after Jesus's birth while most scholars believe Jesus had siblings—four brothers and at least two sisters. Most people would agree that Mary lived her life as a sexually active woman.

An immaculate conception was not an unusual belief during Jesus's times. Non-Jews believed in divine conception in stories about Plato, Alexander the Great, and Augustus Caesar. It also appeared in Greek and Roman mythology.*

Mythology was deeply embedded in the culture during Jesus's times, and it shouldn't be a surprise to anyone that mythology would appear in stories marking the event of the birth of Jesus.

**What about the celebration of Christmas?** History cannot account for the year, month, or even the season or location of his birth. The date chosen had more to do with pagan holidays that were celebrated at the time. Constantine's mother, Helena, identified most of the sites in the holy land associated with the life of Christ with little or no historical basis. The birth of Jesus was not celebrated

---

* Tabor, 44. There are also claims that after learning she was pregnant Mary left town to stay with close family relatives (Elizabeth and Zechariah the parents of John the Baptizer who lived in Ein Kerem).

* Ibid., 59–63. There are references in early writings about Jesus that suggests he was "born of fornication and not divine intervention."

* Liston, Bower, Gibson, Michaels, 54. An immaculate conception was not an unusual belief during Jesus' times. Non-Jews believed in divine conception in stories about Plato, Alexander The Great and Augustus Caesar. It also appeared in Greek and Roman mythology

until the fourth century. It's interesting to note early settlers (pilgrims) outlawed the celebration of Christmas because of the association with paganism. Most people would be surprised to know the celebration of Christmas among Protestants in the United States is a relatively new holiday. It wasn't declared a federal holiday until June 26, 1870.

**What do we know about the life of Jesus before he appeared in Jerusalem at age 33?** Nothing. It's strange that so much is written about the life of Jesus, yet nothing is known about his life from his birth until three years before his untimely death. He left no footprints that anyone can find.

Some people speculate he may have spent time in India, where he was influenced by Buddhism. Those teachings would include his simplicity of life, charity, serving the poor, and forgiveness rather than revenge. They would not have been associated with the Jewish religion at the time. It might account for people wondering where he got those ideas. Anyone who studies Buddhism can surely see the similarities in Jesus's teaching.[*]

Whatever is said about those lost years, it's safe to say he was alive and was being influenced in some way. It's a matter of speculation how he was influenced. That remains a puzzle even among Christians.

Most of what's written about Jesus had to do with his ministry. To add to the confusion, the Gospels don't agree on how long that lasted. Mark, Matthew, and Luke say it lasted a few months, and John says three years.[*]

**Was Jesus married?** There is no evidence in the scriptures to indicate Jesus was married. However, some scholars claim there is a strong probability he was married. Historians say, for Jewish men, non-marriage was an unacceptable way of life during Jesus's time. It was not a question of choice. In the Old Testament, Abraham,

---

[*] *The Unkown Jesus*, Biography Special for A&E Network, Produced by Filmroose Inc., 1999. Jesus's link with Buddhisim.

[*] Ehrman, 40. Mark, Matthew and Luke say it lasted a few months and John says three years.

Moses, and David were all married. The Gospels say all his apostles were married.

At the time, Jesus lived the duties of Jewish fathers for their sons were as follows:

1. Circumcision
2. Redeem the child in the temple
3. Instruct him in the Torah
4. Teach him a trade
5. Arrange a wife*

There are accounts in the Gospels that Joseph did all the above for Jesus and that marriage would have been consistent with the Jewish tradition at the time.

Some scholars speculate he might have been married to Mary Magdalene. In the early years of the church, women were held in low esteem. Pope Gregory the Great (590–604) labeled Mary Magdalene a prostitute. That perception lasted until 1969, when the church corrected the misstatement. Today most biblical scholars view Mary Magdalene as someone who was probably as close to Jesus as any of his male apostles and say there is no evidence she was ever a prostitute. There is some evidence to suggest they may have been lovers. The Gnostic Gospels claim Jesus kissed Mary Magdalene often on the lips.

The church's low regard for women led to the male-dominated institutions we see today in the Catholic Church and among many Protestant churches.

I can understand why those who declared Jesus divine didn't want him to possess the human frailties associated with marriage or sex. It wouldn't be godly or Christlike. On the other hand, it can be argued he was a fully equipped man of the flesh. Based on claims of there being an absence of any female intimacy by Jesus, I'm surprised someone hasn't suggested he might have been gay. That's a thought that could turn the Christian world upside down.

---

* *The Unknown Jesus*, Strong probability he was married and the reasons.

**What about Jesus the healer and other miracles?** In regard to the thirty-five miracles in the Gospels such as healing the sick, raising the dead, turning water into wine, and walking on water, etc., some followers claim they're facts and should be taken literally. Others say they're metaphors and should be taken figuratively. There's no documented evidence outside the scriptures to prove they ever occurred. Most scholars believe those who wrote about them were not eyewitnesses. They came from the oral history that was passed down over time to promote the Jesus movement and have to be accepted on faith. There's some contradictions in the New Testament about why Jesus performed the miracles. John claims he performed them to convince people to believe in him.* Matthew claims he didn't perform miracles to prove himself but only to help those in need.* Paul doesn't recount any of the miracles.*

**What did Jesus look like?** The depiction of Jesus that we see on the crucifixion and in pictures adorning churches and homes don't accurately represent the way he looked. Those depictions were created by Renaissance painters who created him in their own likeness. It was the way people in the Western world wanted him to appear, blond hair and blue eyes. Forensic medical artists have recently used modern scientific methods to recreate his appearance based on what people looked like during his time in that region. That would be short, dark hair, dark eyes, dark complexion, prominent nose, and a broad face. He looked like many of the Arabs living in the region today.*

---

* Ehrman 84. "John claims he performed them to convince people to believe in him."

* Ibid. 84. "Matthew claims he didn't perform miracles to prove himself but only to help those in need."

* Barker, 368. Paul doesn't recount any of the miracles.

* Jeremy Bowen, et. al. *Jesus the Complete Story*, BBC video (2001) aired on the Discover Channel. Forensic medical artists have recently used modern scientific methods to recreate his appearance based on what people looked like during his time in that region. That would be short, dark hair, dark eyes dark complection, prominent nose, and a broad face. He looked like many of the Arabs living in the region today.

This is not a significant issue. I just find this misconception interesting to point out. I'm sure it won't change how the church and the Western world will continue depicting him. Among most religions, old ideas and beliefs change slowly, if at all. They don't let facts get in the way of what they want to believe. Many of my Christian friends tell me that historical accuracy is not important since Christianity is built on faith. That's probably true for many Christians.

**What about the resurrection?** The main claim Christians make as proof Jesus was the Son of God is the resurrection. Without that claim, his life would have had much less meaning to future generations and could have meant the end of the Jesus movement.

Today if someone finds a body missing, it's assumed it was moved. That's what Tabor speculates about Jesus's body in his book, *The Jesus Dynasty.* He suggests the body was probably moved by his family.

Since Jesus and his family were Jews who followed all the customs associated with the Jewish tradition, it stands to reason they would follow Jewish customs when it came to the death of Jesus. The Jewish tradition required that a corpse must be buried within twenty-four hours after the death. Since Jesus's body had been rushed to a temporary tomb because of the Passover holiday, it makes sense that the family would want to complete his burial as soon as possible. That would have included washing and anointing his body.* Since Mary, the mother of Jesus, and other members of his family were present during his crucifixion and his death, it's entirely possible they would have wanted to prepare his body, remove it from the temporary tomb, and place him in a final resting place. The area around the site where he was crucified is filled with ancient tombs from around the time of Jesus.

---

* Tabor, 235. The Jewish tradition required that a corpse must be buried within twenty-four hours after the death. Since Jesus's body had been rushed to a temporary tomb because of the Passover holiday it makes sense that the family would want to complete his burial as soon as possible. That would have included washing and anointing his body.

A look at the biblical accounts of the risen Christ makes the event of his resurrection seem even more unbelievable. Tabor claims the story first appeared in a letter written by Paul to the 1 Corinthians in AD 54.* He goes on to say the original version of the gospel of Mark says nothing about his resurrection and appearances after his death. His account ends with the empty tomb.* He claims scribes who copied Mark made up the ending that appears in Mark some three hundred years after the original text was composed.* This is verifiable. He goes on to explain since Matthew and Luke used Mark as their source and were written forty to seventy years after the death of Jesus by people who were not likely original witnesses of the event, their claim of Jesus's resurrection most likely came from Paul, who got his information from an alleged vision of the risen Christ.

To add more doubt about the claim of the risen Christ and sightings, the versions of that event from John, Matthew, and Luke's are different. "They don't agree as to who arrived first at the tomb and what subsequently transpired."* I would challenge anyone to come up with one account of the resurrection by using the Gospels. It can't be done.

Most people view the crucifixion as an event that was unique to the death of Jesus. The execution by crucifixion was a common practice by Romans during Jesus's times. He was one of thousands of people who met their fate by dying on the cross. It was probably a daily event in the holy lands during Jesus's time. That's not to diminish the way Jesus died. It was probably one of the cruelest way to execute people ever devised by man.

---

* Ibid., 231. Tabor claims the story first appeared in a letter written by Paul to the 1 Corinthians in ad 54.

* The original version of the Gospel of Mark says nothing about his resurrection and appearances after his death. His account ends with the empty tomb.

* 231. Scribes who copied Mark made up the ending that appears in Mark some three hundred years after the original text was composed.

* 228–229. The versions of that event from John, Matthew and Luke's are different. "They don't agree as to who arrived first at the tomb and what subsequently transpired."

**Where did the puritanical elements come from?** The puritanical influence found its way into the Christian movement with Martin Luther and John Calvin during the Protestant Reformation. They were influenced by the writings of St. Augustine (354–430 CE). St. Augustine lived the first part of his life in sin before becoming a born-again Christian. In later life, he came to believe that to take pleasure in sex was evil and sinful and should only be practiced for the purpose of reproduction. He wrote:

> *Although your eyes may chance to rest upon some woman or other, you must not fix your gaze upon any woman. Seeing women when you go out is not forbidden, but it is sinful to desire them or to wish them to desire you, for it is not by tough or passionate feeling alone but by one's gaze also that lustful desires mutually arise. And do not say that your hearts are pure if there is immodesty of the eye, because the unchaste eye carries the message of an impure heart. And when such hearts disclose their unchaste desires in a mutual gaze, even without saying a word, then it is that chastity that suddenly goes out of their life, even though their bodies remain unsullied by unchaste acts.*[*]

Today most people would consider St. Augustine's statements totally unrealistic and unattainable considering the basic nature of men and women. Yet one does not have to look far to see elements of that message in many of today's fundamental Christian churches. It's ironic that the Old Testament is full of sexual promiscuity, including mistresses and concubines. I'm not sure how that gets reconciled, but it does. While there is some basis for those puritanical beliefs in the New Testament, they appeared to have been dormant until the Protestant Reformation. Today they're well ingrained in many funda-

---

[*] *The Rule of St. Augustine*, n.d., http://www.geocities.com/Athens/1534/ruleaug.html#Moderation%20and%20Self%20Denial (5 May 2004).

mental Protestant churches. It's another example of how people and their movements have changed Christianity.

Today some fundamental Christians have taken their puritanical attitudes about sex to the extreme. For example, even though the United States has one of the highest teenage pregnancy rates than any other industrialized country, many fundamental Christians oppose sex education. They also oppose the use of condoms in countries that are being ravished by the HIV virus resulting in millions of unwanted children and unnecessary deaths because they believe condoms promote promiscuity. Some even oppose the use of the human papilloma virus vaccine (HPV) in young girls, which is now the most common sexually transmitted disease in the United States and is the leading cause of cervical cancer. It's estimated that each year, five thousand women die of cervical cancer in this country. The vaccine is safe and effective, yet some fundamental Christians have successfully blocked its use because they believe the existence of the HPV virus helps reduce premarital sex. I think most rational and informed people would agree that sex education is better than ignorance, condoms are better than unsafe sex, and the HPV vaccine is better than cervical cancer.

*Conclusion*

It's easy to see that while Christians think everything they believe emanates directly from Christ, a look at the evolution of Christianity shows how people and events have defined and shaped those beliefs. Christianity is not what it was nor is it what it will become. It's ever-changing albeit sometimes extremely slow.

What is known about the life of Jesus occurred two thousand years ago and was passed down by word of mouth for thirty to 125 years before being written and later translated into different languages. No originals of the four gospels have ever been found. Some of what was known could have been significantly changed in those early translations. We also know that like most historical figures, their legends grow larger with the passage of time.

We know the people who passed down his story were not impartial. They were biased and fallible. They promoted their version of his life to appeal to different audiences at different times. They often went to great lengths to link Jesus with the prophesies in the Old Testament. More than likely it led to exaggerations, distortions, and stories that were made up to substantiate their claims. A close scrutiny of what they wrote reveals a host of flaws and contradiction. What they said is just as significant as what they omitted.

To add to the problem, the early church went to great lengths to diminish the humanity of Jesus and Mary by emphasizing their divinity. In doing that, they placed needless hurdles in the way of scholars, making it more difficult for them to find the historical Jesus.

Based on my studies, I believe there's no historical evidence supporting the divinity of Jesus. What we know about him is based on what the early church determined to be true 325 years after his death at the First Ecumenical Council in Nicaea. Who's to say they got it right? To prevent others from learning about other versions of Jesus, all early Christian sects were banished and all other beliefs about him were forbidden. The church's accounts are full of contradictions. Much of what is believed about Jesus came from Paul, who didn't know Jesus when he was alive and attributes his claims to alleged visions. Paul had a huge influence over the gospel writers, but that doesn't mean they all agreed. Their writings contain different accounts linking Jesus with God, along with two different accounts of the virgin birth. Two of the gospel writers omit his birth altogether. The virgin birth reads like the mythology that was popular during the time of Jesus. It was the mission of the church to spread those beliefs, gaining untold power and wealth. There is no historical basis supporting his resurrection and the claim he's the Son of God. The accounts of his resurrection are so different even the faithful can't construct the event from the Gospels without running into contradictions. The resurrection belief most likely came from Paul in a letter he wrote to the 1 Corinthians in AD 54. The date of his birth was made up, so Christians would have something to celebrate during pagan holidays. His appearance was created by Renaissance painters, so he would resemble Western Europeans. After the Reformation, thousands of sects spun off the Catholic Church, creating disagreements and different beliefs. Over the years, people and their movements have shaped what most people believe about Jesus. All this should at least raise reasonable doubt by anyone searching for the truth. For all these reasons and more it takes a giant leap of faith to believe what we're told about Jesus by Christian churches. Of course, that's true about all religions that base their beliefs on what people said about God two thousand to three thousand years ago.

Even though Christianity's claims are based on faith and aren't considered verifiable by historical standards, it's not surprising that they were embraced during ancient times and survive today. For like no other religion, it accepts that we all live in sin and promises everlasting life to its believers. It appealed to the masses and gave hope to the hopeless and continues to serve that need today.

One of the reasons Christianity has survived and grown is that its followers were told if they didn't believe Jesus was the son of God and died for their sins, they would go to hell. That message kept a great many people in the fold and provided an incentive for others to take up the faith. It continues to be a major reason for its grip on people today.

In summary, it can be said Christianity has undergone a great many changes over the last two thousand years and will continue to change as the world and its people evolve. Today there are thirty-four thousand Christian denominations worldwide* and 1,200 in the US reflecting differences in what Christians believe. Its fluidity has often been used to promote a wide range of positions and contradictions, such as war and peace: turn thy cheek (forgiveness) versus an eye for an eye (revenge); pro-life versus capital punishment; slavery versus antislavery; homophobia versus gays being children of God; support for women versus subservient to men and opposition to their presence in the church hierarchy. The list is never-ending. It can be said almost any position can be supported based on how people choose to interpret and cherry-pick the Scriptures.

---

* "Religions of the World: Numbers of Adherents; names of houses of worship; names of leaders; rates of growth…," n.d., http://www.religioustolerance.org/rel_rate.htm. (3 February 2004) 34,000 different Christian denominations throughout the worldwide.

I've included a few passages Christians seldom point to when promoting their faith even though it's a common evangelical belief that all scripture is inspired by God and is equally authoritative.

[Hagar and Ishmael:] *Now Sarai, Abram's wife, had borne him no children. But she had an Egyptian maidservant named Hagar; so she said to Abram, "The L*ORD *has kept me from having children. Go, sleep with my maidservant; perhaps I can build a family through her." Abram agreed to what Sarai said.* (Genesis 16:2)

[Punishment for nonbelievers:] *If your very own brother, or your son or daughter, or the wife you love, or your closest friend secretly entices you, saying, "Let us go and worship other gods" (gods that neither you nor your fathers have known, gods of the peoples around you, whether near or far, from one end of the land to the other), do not yield to him or listen to him. Show him no pity. Do not spare him or shield him. You must certainly put him to death. Your hand must be the first in putting him to death, and then the hands of all the people. Stone him to death, because he tried to turn you away from the* L*ORD... (Deuteronomy 13:6–10)

[The Sabbath:] *For six days, work is to be done, but the seventh day shall be your holy day, a Sabbath of rest to the L*ORD*. Whoever does any work on it must be put to death.* (Exodus 35:2)

[Rebellious son:] *If a man has a stubborn and rebellious son who does not obey his father and mother and will not listen to them when they discipline him, his father and mother shall take hold of him and bring him to the elders at the gate of his town. They shall say to the elders, "This son of ours is stubborn and rebellious. He will not obey us. He is a profligate and a drunkard." Then all the men of his town shall stone him to death. You must purge the evil from among you. All Israel will hear of it and be afraid.* (Deuteronomy 21:18–21)

*Anyone who curses his father or mother must be put to death.* (Exodus 21:17)

[Slavery:] *As for your male and female slaves whom you may have: you may buy male and female slaves from among the nations that are round you. You may also buy from among strangers who sojourn with you and their families that are with you, who have been born in our hand; and they may be your property. You may bequeath them to your sons after you, to inherit as a possession forever…* (Leviticus 25:44–46)

[Marrying a captive woman:] *When you go to war against your enemies and the LORD your God delivers them into your hands and you take captives, if you notice among the captives a beautiful woman and are attracted to her, you may take her as your wife. Bring her into your home and have her shave her head, trim her nails and put aside the clothes she was wearing when captured. After she has lived in your house and mourned her father and mother for a full month, then you may go to her and be her husband and she shall be your wife. If you are not pleased with her, let her go wherever she wishes. You must not sell her or treat her as a slave, since you have dishonored her.* (Deuteronomy 21:10–14)

[Adultery:] *If a man commits adultery with another man's wife—with the wife of his neigh-*

> *bor—both the adulterer and the adulteress must be*
> *put to death.* (Leviticus 20:10)

Some might say the Old Testament passages don't reflect Christian beliefs. I would argue that most Christian churches make frequent references to the Old Testament in their services. Furthermore, no Christian can deny the Old Testament gives credence to the divinity of Christ by claiming he fulfilled Old Testament prophesies. Christianity will forever be intertwined in the Old Testament and wouldn't exist without it.

Others argue those passages pertain to a different time period. If true, how does anyone know what passages apply to what time periods? There's no mention of that anywhere in the Bible. Besides, some of these statements are so repulsive they shouldn't pertain to any time period. I see that argument as nothing more than a feeble attempt to explain away passages no one in their right mind could support.

It could be argued the New Testament is even more wicked than the Old Testament because of its emphasis on hell. In the Old Testament, hell is just death or the grave. The Christian hell is eternal damnation and suffering. Many fundamental Christians condemn people to hell who don't accept the divinity of Christ and the Gospels being the Word of God. Some even condemn people to hell who are of the same faith but don't adhere to their particular teachings. Christianity didn't invent the concept of hell, but it did put its unique spin on it. It's mentioned more than heaven in the New Testament. I'll never understand how people who believe in a loving God could embrace such an evil belief.

Besides the emphasis on hell, there are a number of passages in the New Testament that Christians avoid quoting. Here are a few examples:

> [Punishment for nonbelievers:] *If a man*
> *abide not in me, he is cast forth as a branch, and is*
> *withered: and men gather them, and cast them into*
> *fire, and they are burned.* (John 15:6)

[Lust and adultery:] *Everyone who looks at a woman with lust in his heart has already committed adultery with her...* (Matthew 5:28–30)

*Whoever marries a divorced women commits adultery.* (Matthew 5:31)

[Public display of faith:] *Beware of practicing your piety before others in order to be seen by them; for then you have no reward from Father in heaven...wherever you pray, go into the room and shut the door and pray to your Father who sees in secret will reward you.* (Sermon on the Mount, Matthew 6:1–6)

Most evangelical Christians go out of their way to display their faith in public.

[Wealth:] *It's easier for a camel to go through the eye of a needle than for a rich man to enter the kingdom of God.* (Matthew 19:24)

You cannot serve God and wealth...

*Do not store up yourselves treasure on earth, where moth and rust consume and where thieves break in and steal; but store up for yourselves treasures in heaven, where neither moth nor rust consumes and where thieves do not break in and steal... Do not worry about your life, what you will eat or what you will drink, or about your body, what you will wear. Is not life more than food, and the body, more than cloths?* (Sermon of the Mount, Matthew 6:19, 25)

Luke expresses his sentiment in another way:

*From everyone to whom much has been given,
much will be required; and from one to whom
much as been trusted, even more will be expected.*
(Luke 12:48)

People of faith who believe everything in their holy books as being literally true usually represent the radical branch of their faith. The vast majority of people seldom embrace a literal interpretation of the Gospels. In the end, we all choose to believe what we want to believe, and in most cases, it has little to do with the facts, truth, logic, or common sense.

Jesus's view of material wealth should make many of today's Christians feel uncomfortable. He lived like a nomad and told his disciples to give up everything and take up a life of self-imposed poverty. Most church leaders today wouldn't think of living that kind of life. Today's clerics see no problem taking money from their parishioners to support a lifestyle that's often better than their followers. I also wonder what Jesus would think about the huge ornate cathedrals and churches built in his name. How does all that get reconciled with today's Christians? When I look at the Christian movement today, I often ask myself, What would Jesus think?

According to Albert Schweitzer, "We all find the Jesus we want because we know so little about him." I'd like to digress into the world of fantasy and speculate on what I think Jesus would have been like had he returned to earth during my lifetime.

First I would say he's one of the historical figures I would most like to spend time with if that were possible. Of course, my Christian friends say that's entirely possible. To move on, we know he was a religious scholar with radical ideas. He was also a political activist. Those are two qualities I admire in people today. We also know he didn't spend time with the rich and powerful but with the poor, the weak, and the downtrodden. They were the kind of people most of society still likes to ignore or avoid even today.

It's my feeling had he returned during my lifetime, he would have been more comfortable living with the hippies during the '60s and demonstrating against the war in Vietnam rather than sitting in a Southern Baptist Church or volunteering to give the commencement address at Bob Jones University. I even think he would have rejoiced in the free love movement. He and his followers would be labeled hippies based on their communal lifestyle, self-imposed poverty, their antiestablishment rebellious attitude, and their dress (robes and sandals). He was a hell raiser in his time, and I don't think he'd be any different today. I'm sure he would have been active in the Civil Rights Movement and would have been seen marching with Martin Luther King. He probably would have been incarcerated several times. In today's time, I believe he'd be marching with the gay and lesbian groups. He'd probably be a dues-paying member of Greenpeace and not a registered Republican. I'm sure he'd be upset with many Christians for what they've done in his name. He'd be especially upset about people using his name to solicit money for their personal comfort and well-being.

I think most Christians today would have trouble relating to him. He wouldn't be the Christ they've come to identify with in their church. They'd probably jeer him and oppose many of the causes he'd represent. He probably wouldn't be welcome in their houses of worship. His rebellious attitude and Middle Eastern appearance would probably put him on the "no fly list." Since Jesus never claimed to be anything but a Jew, he'd be more comfortable worshiping in a synagogue. He'd tell Christians they were violating the Ten Commandments by worshiping a false god (meaning him). He'd be appalled at their use of graven images. He'd claim to be nothing more than a Jewish political activist with an inspirational message who promoted a Jewish uprising and was crucified by the Romans and not the Jews. He'd be much better than the judgmental Jesus I've come to know from my Christian friends. The question I'd most like to ask him is where did he go during those thirty lost years, and what was he doing? I think we'd all be surprised with his answer.

I admit most of what I said about Jesus is speculation, but that's true about everything that's said about him. All anyone can do is speculate. Christians have faith they're right. I continue to question.

# Observations and Myth Busting

*Like most people, I used to think God was synonymous with religion. I don't think that's true. I believe if there's a God, he's not a Christian, Muslim, Jew, Buddhist, or any other religion devised by man. He's just God. I believe he'll accept people of all faiths and people of no faith. If we're judged, I'd like to believe it'll be based on whether we lived a righteous life rather than our choice of religions. If by chance heaven is the exclusive domain for evangelicals or some other like-minded group, I'm not sure that's where I want to spend eternity. I've always valued diversity… Christianity's core beliefs may be well-meaning, but their followers are often misguided by their church. From my point of view, there has to be a better way to identify with the meaning of life and our relationship with others. Christianity has far too many trappings for me to embrace.*

—Al Vercellino

While living my life in a Christian country and community, I devoted a great deal of my time observing how Christians were dealing with their lives and how some churches dealt with some of our most pressing social issues. I also took notice of how Christianity fared in terms of tolerance for others who held different beliefs and its general goodness. Too often I found Christianity falling short of being a positive force in promoting human rights and being on the "right" side of many social issues. The reader will see my quarrel is not with God or Christ but with his followers.

My search led me to the following issues:

**What does it mean to be a Christian?** Throughout my life I've been a curious observer of the different beliefs held by Christians.

While living in a Christian Reformed community (Grand Rapids, Michigan in the mid-1960s), I learned they took their Sunday Sabbath seriously by not shopping or even doing yard work. Some even tried to impose that religious practice on the community. As a school administrator, I encountered Christian groups wanting the school to remove what most people considered to be harmless books they said violated their fundamental beliefs. There were Christians who even wanted to censor what I watched or read in my own home. Some thought almost anything having to do with sex was shameful. I met Christians who viewed homosexuals as a threat to their religion and country. I knew Christians who sent their kids to Bob Jones University, where racial bigotry flourished. I read that Southern Baptist missionaries were told they had until May 5, 2003, to swear belief in wives' submission to husbands along with opposition to any female pastors. I also met Christians who were "normal" mainstream Americans without any unusual or extreme religious beliefs. What puzzled me is that they all received their information from the same source but somehow arrived at different conclusions about what it means to be a Christian.

I came to understand there were two distinct groups of Christians, moderate and fundamental. While many fall somewhere within the continuum, the two groups have different ideas about what it means to be a Christian.

Moderate Christians don't define themselves by their faith. Many call themselves Christians out of convenience. It's the religion they inherited from their families. They might not even attend church. They embrace what they believe is the "goodness" associated with their faith while placing less emphasis on doctrine or mystical beliefs. They're not hampered by church dogma in making decisions about the important social issues. They're free thinkers who use common sense and follow their conscience in determining what to believe. They don't use their religion to judge others. They represent the majority of people who call themselves Christians.

Fundamental Christians like to talk about their faith to anyone who will listen. They proselytize and like quoting scripture. They're sometimes judgmental and often hold prejudicial feelings about people who don't share in their beliefs. They claim not to be prejudiced by saying they represent "God's Word," that being, "the absolute truth." They claim not to judge but are quick to say how God judges. They often claim to have the absolute truth from God. They're not free thinkers. They believe what their church tells them to believe. I call it "group think." They represent about one-third of the Christian faith in America.

When moderate Christians select a church, it's usually because of family tradition. They're views are more compatible with a more liberal point of view in regard to social issues. Their social life isn't restricted to the members of their congregation.

Fundamental Christians often join a church based on their interpretation of the Scriptures and define themselves by their church affiliation. Most of their social life revolves around the members of their congregation. They often dwell on their personal salvation and use each other to reinforce their views, values, and lifestyle. They're slow to accept social change. Some could be described as living a cultlike existence. They might be well intentioned, but in my opinion, I find they're often misguided by their church.

I plead guilty of generalizing about moderate and fundamental Christians, but I don't think I'm entirely wrong in my description of the two groups. We need only look at the polarization within our political landscape to see that our nation is divided by extreme elements that have their roots in religious beliefs.

**What about the power of prayer?** My Christian friends often use their belief in the power of prayer to support their belief in God. The power of prayer is not without some merit. However, like all claims of faith, it doesn't prove there's a god or that he intervenes in our behalf.

I think the belief in prayer stems from the need some people have to believe in a higher power that watches over them and makes them feel loved and secure in an insecure and sometimes frightening world. I liken it to hearkening back to our early years when most of us had parents who fulfilled that role.

When people claim prayers work, I think it has more to do with the power of the mind than God's intervention. When we face life-threatening situations involving our health or physical well-being, we have a choice of giving in to the threat or fighting. Those who have hope will likely have a better chance of survival than those who don't. Prayer is an expression of that kind of hope. It produces a positive force. Whether people attribute it to prayer or the mind's will to overcome a crisis, the results are the same. The mind is a powerful tool that probably has more potential in affecting our life outcomes than we currently understand.

The placebo effect in medical trials is an example of how the mind can affect our physical state. It's not unusual for people who are given a placebo, rather than a drug, to show signs of improvement. Studies show as many as a third of the patients in clinical trials who take placebos and not the drug being tested get better. This is particularly true with conditions such as pain or depression.* That's why good medical trials use large, randomized, placebo-controlled, double-blinded techniques when testing drugs. The same methods should also be applied when conducting studies on prayer.

Most of the claims about prayers are anecdotal or personal testimonials and not the result of sound scientific methods. There have only been a few scientific studies on the power of prayer that meet the strict adherence to sound research. The one that stands out was conducted by Dr. Herbert Benson, a cardiologist at the Mind/Body Medical Institute near Boston and reported in the *American Heart Journal* of April 2006. It found no difference between those patients who were prayed for and those who were not. In fact, those who were prayed for, and knew it, did a little worse.*

---

* Jerry Adler, "A Big Dose of Skepticism" (Newsweek, December 10, 2007), 22. Studies show that it's not unusual for a third of the patients in clinical trials who take placebos and not the drug being tested to get better. This is particularly true with conditions such as pain or depression.

* 23 H. Benson et al., "Study of the therapeutic effects of intercessory prayer (STEP) in cardiac bypass patients," *American Heart Journal* 151:4 (April 2006): 934–942. It found no difference between those patients who were prayed for and those who were not. In fact, those who were prayed for, and knew it, did a little worse.

I'm always amazed when people talk about miracles taking place when they pray at religious sites known for their divine healing power. I'm sure healing occurs on occasion, but if one were to consider the hundreds of thousands of people who visit those sites who are not cured, the few who claim they were healed would be no different from the healing that occurs in any random sample of the same number of people who didn't visit the site. It's interesting to note no one has ever known God to cure amputees. I've always wondered what the faithful would say about that observation.

Unexplained medical cures have always occurred. The fact that they can't always be explained doesn't prove God's intervention. In time, the medical community will probably have those answers.

Those who argue that payers work usually cite examples as proof. When people survive a serious illness, they say God answered their prayers. When a tragedy strikes, leaving some to survive while killing others, I hear those who survive say God was looking out for them. Does that mean God wasn't looking out for those who didn't survive? There's never a good answer, but the one I hear most often when it doesn't work out is that it wasn't in God's will. They'll say, "God works in mysterious ways, and it's not for us to know." While that kind of thinking defies logic, it nonetheless shows how people of faith reason. They claim to be right no matter the outcome.

When people face a serious health problem, most rational people place their faith in finding the best doctors and the latest medical treatments. Faith plays a secondary role. If the faithful believed prayer was the answer, there would be no need for doctors or medical advances. It would always be left in God's hand. When people take faith to that extreme and reject medical treatment, others label them as irrational extremists.

Prayer is not unlike meditation. Most experts would agree meditation has health benefits. It can reduce stress, blood pressure, and other kinds of physical ailments. Some claim it can add years to our lives. They're probably right.

Everyone knows prayers have their limits. Regardless what we believe, we're all destined to die, and all the praying in the world won't change that. The last I heard Christians were dying at the same rate as non-Christians.

**Were our founding fathers devout Christians and are we a Christian nation?** Contrary to what the Christian right would have us believe, not all our founding fathers were devout Christians. They were influenced more by the ideas of the enlightenment and the philosophies of Hume, Locke, Rousseau, Voltaire, and Kant rather than Jesus. They were more likely to be Deists (not believing in a personal god) or Unitarian. That would include Franklin, Jefferson, Madison, Monroe, and some historians also include Washington.* Thomas Jefferson went so far as to cut out all the mystical sections in his Bible, leaving only the moral teachings of Christ. They supported religion for the masses because they believed it played a central role in promoting morality, order, and stability. Some were devote Christians like Patrick Henry, John Jay, and Samuel Adams. While not a founding father, Abraham Lincoln was well-versed in Scripture but didn't embrace the concept of a personal God and life after death. He seldom attended church.

They weren't too far removed from a time when the early settlers came to America to escape religious persecution and then established colonies that had little or no tolerance for people who didn't share in their beliefs such as the Puritans in New England. Nine of the original thirteen colonies had state-established churches during the colonial period. They learned from the country's short history that true liberty cannot exist in a church-run state. Leaving God out of government and the Constitution was one of the most significant contributions they made in support of individual liberty. It's still considered to be the hallmark of our great American experiment.

The establishment clause in Article 1 of our Constitution states, "Congress shall make no law respecting the establishment of religion or prohibiting the free exercise thereof." The separation of church and state was advanced even further in 1802, when Thomas Jefferson

---

* David L Holmes. *The Faiths of the Founding Fathers* (Oxford, New York: Oxford University Press, 2006), 50–51. That would include Franklin, Washington, Jefferson, Madison, and Monroe.

wrote his famous letter to the Danbury Baptist Association where he refers to "the wall of the separation between church and state." The Baptists were delighted with Jefferson's answer. The matter referred to a system of religious taxation that forced many Connecticut Baptists to support the established Congregationalist Church. It reinforced the principle of religious freedom.

We can also look at the first treaty signed by the United States after we became a nation. It states, "The United States is not in any sense founded on a Christian religion." This was the Tripoli Peace Treaty that was started under President Washington, ratified by Congress with no objections, and signed by President Adams in 1779. While we are a nation with a large population of Christians, we are not a Christian nation.

While we hold dearly to the concept of the separation of church and state, we also acknowledge a public religion. The generic name Jefferson called "Creator" and "Nature of God" in the Deceleration of Independence. It also includes many of the religious symbols we see adorning many of our public buildings. It acknowledges the role religion has played in our country but makes no attempt to promote any one religion over another. When a president says, "God bless America," each American is free to define God in whatever way he chooses. While religious extremists have attempted to make Christianity the official religion of the US, their attempts have always met with failure.

As a result of our religious freedom, we've become the most religious nation in the western hemisphere. It's allowed all religions to compete and flourish without government interference.

Today many on the Christian right would like to blur the lines between the separation of church and state. We see this with issues relating to gays, stem cell research, school prayer, and abortion. Those are all issues worthy of debate. Unfortunately, a civil dialogue is sometimes impossible when one party claims to represent the views of God and no other opinions matter. In my opinion, the Christian right would be better served trying to change the hearts and minds of people rather than trying to legislate morality. If we've learned anything from our past, it would be that legislating morality doesn't work.

The Christian right tries to exert undue influence by voting as a block. They call themselves "value" voters. I contend everyone is a "value" voter. I don't expect people to leave their religious views and convictions outside the voting booth, but I also believe democracy would be better served if more people based their vote on all the issues facing our nation rather than focusing on a few narrow religious issues such as abortion, school prayer, and homosexuality. Some examples of broader issues include war, global warming, energy independence, health care, education, poverty, immigration reform, saving Social Security and Medicare, finding a cure for cancer and other deadly diseases, reducing the widening disparity between the rich and poor, eliminating government waste, balancing the budget, excessive special interest influence, overhauling our tax code, and a dysfunctional government as evidenced by the gridlock in Washington. Those are all issues that if not properly addressed will lead to our demise as a great nation.

**What role did Christianity play in slavery, Jim Crow and the Civil Rights Movement?** My Christian friends like to say Christians opposed slavery, Jim Crow laws, and championed the Civil Rights Movement. That might be partially true, but it's not the whole story. Christianity is too intertwined in our culture to not share significant responsibility for how Blacks were mistreated during most of our country's existence.

Slavery found its way into the New World with the settlement of Jamestown. It became ingrained in the fabric of our country even in the North and remained an integral part of the Southern culture and economy until the end of the Civil War. One in seven people was owned by someone else because of the color of their skin. Many were treated no differently than farm animals. It resulted in family members being separated for life after being sold. Their lives were so hard less than four out of one hundred lived to be sixty years old. Most slave owners were "God-fearing Christians." Twelve of our first fifteen presidents were slave owners. We were the last major country to end slavery, and that didn't happen without one of the most violent struggles in the history of mankind. The war divided families and resulted in the deaths of 620,000 Americans. While we take pride in saying we fought the Civil War to end slavery, we can't deny almost half the Americans killed in that conflict were Southern Whites, mostly Christians, who died trying to defend slavery. As a side note, Russia peacefully ended serfdom before we ended slavery. The only two countries that still had slavery prior to the Civil War were Cuba and Brazil.

Contrary to popular belief, the Civil War was not about freeing slaves in the South. It was about whether the new territories in the West would be free states or slave states. At the beginning of the war, Lincoln made it clear his goal was not to abolish slavery in the South. His goal was to keep the Union together. He didn't issue the Emancipation Proclamation until the war was well underway. The reason he delayed was that he feared losing support of his solders if they thought they were fighting for Blacks. At the time, the Emancipation Proclamation was a courageous act and not well accepted by everyone in the North.

The earliest supporters of the abolitionist movement were the peace-loving Quakers. While many in the North supported freeing the slaves, they didn't embrace giving them social and economic equality. That didn't begin to happen until the mid-twentieth century. Blacks represented a dilemma for most Americans. Most people, including Christians, were not eager to assimilate Blacks into their White culture. Prior to the Emancipation Proclamation, the popular answer to the problem of Blacks in America was to send them back to Africa or some other place where they would be out of sight. Even Lincoln contemplated that idea prior to signing the Emancipation Proclamation.

Christians who supported slavery found the Bible to be a convenient cover. For example, the Bible states:

> *As for your male and female slaves whom you may have: you may buy male and female slaves from among the nations that are round you. You may also buy from among strangers who sojourn*

*with you and their families that are with you, who have been born in our hand; and they may be your property. You may bequeath them to your sons after you, to inherit as a possession forever...* (Leviticus 25:44–46)

*Slaves, be obedient to those who are your earthly masters, with fear and trembling, in singleness of heart, as to Christ...* (Ephesians 6:5)

The Old Testament supports slavery, and there's no place in the New Testament where Jesus denounces the practice.* The only difference is that during biblical times, slaves were the result of wars and conquests. It wasn't a matter of race. I would argue using the color of one's skin to single out slaves makes it even more evil. If the vast majority of Christians opposed slavery, it wouldn't have lasted as long as it did.

Slavery ended with the Civil War but was replaced with another sinister plot to keep Blacks in their place. They were called Jim Crow laws. Good Southern White Christians used their power to keep Blacks from achieving social and economic equality by segregation, relegating them to the most menial jobs, giving them little in the way of educational opportunities, and preventing them from voting. They were intimidated and kept in place by the Ku Klux Klan. Lynching was not uncommon and sometimes even took on the appearance of community entertainment in the town square. Congress never passed an anti-lynching law because of the political clout of the Southern Democrats. That period lasted one hundred years. We can only wonder how that could be possible in a country that prides itself on being a nation of Christians dedicated to freedom, justice, and love.

In the mid-1950s and 1960s, the Civil Rights Movement began. I was in school, but I have vivid memories of those times. I'll never forget seeing good churchgoing Christians and ministers on television using the Scriptures to promote racial intolerance, bigotry, and segregation. They opposed integration because it was against God's

---

*

law and led to the "mixing of seed." Many thought the Black race was inferior to the White race. They used the Bible to justify their racist agenda. I admit most of those people were from the South, or what's commonly called the Bible Belt. Many were Southern Baptists, who make up the nation's largest Protestant denomination. Even though there were Christians supporting the Civil Rights Movement, the strongest opponents came from fundamental Christians. Their use of God and the Bible to promote intolerance didn't endear me to the Christian faith. Sadly, other Christian churches and Christian leaders did little to challenge their conservative Christian brothers about their position. In my opinion, there was an absence of positive vocal leadership from White Christian church leaders. That really bothered me. I expected more from people preaching God's love.

Racial bigotry was not something unique to the South. When I was growing up in the suburbs of Detroit, I remember my parents and other adults saying Blacks were okay so long as they knew their place. Black ghetto neighborhoods were a common sight in the late '40s and early '50s. Racism was more subtle than in the South but just as hurtful. Most of the people who felt that way about Blacks called themselves Christians. They were the Christians of their time. Sadly, there was a silent acceptance of those attitudes among most of the White clergy. That was my world as a young child just as it was for others who lived in the Detroit area, where there was a long history of racism and de facto segregation. Most people are surprised when I tell them George Wallace won the Michigan Democratic presidential primary in 1972. Recently, Donald Trump won the state in the 2016 presidential race against Hillary Clinton. Michigan and other Midwest states are not without its share of bigoted "rednecks."

During the Civil Rights Movement, Christianity played an important role with Martin Luther King and his Southern Christian Leadership Conference. I'm sure without the involvement of Southern Black churches, the movement wouldn't have inspired the commitment Blacks needed to overcome the overwhelming social and institutional obstacles.

It's interesting to note that long after equal rights for Blacks was commonly accepted by the end of the twentieth century, there were still many conservative White Christian churches that opposed interracial marriages based on their interpretation of the Scriptures. It took the Supreme Court in *Love v. Virginia* in 1967 to declare anti-miscegenation laws unconstitutional. At the time, sixteen states still had laws against interracial marriage on their books.

Some might disagree with my claims about the role Christianity played in suppressing equal rights for Blacks. It's a debate that can be argued by either side. Yet I don't think anyone would deny that the strongest opponents of equal rights for Blacks were Southern White Christians from the most religious section of our country. Today all groups do their best to distance themselves from any responsibility for the way our country treated Blacks. Regardless of what anyone chooses to believe, the truth is what it is.

I've asked myself, How could people claiming to represent God be so wrong when it comes to the issue of race? I would have thought that if God spoke to someone during ancient times, he would have told them slavery was wrong.

*What do fundamental Christians believe about other religions?* One of the most significant events in my early search for truth in Christianity was the day a fundamental Christian minister visited my home to talk to me about his faith. This was in the mid-1960s.

I listened with interest but was soon shocked when he said, "God loves you, but if you don't believe Christ died for our sins, you're going to hell." He went on to say that everlasting life can only be achieved through the acceptance of Christ.

I asked, "Does that mean two-thirds of the world's population (non-Christian) were going to hell?"

He said, "Yes," and then added even some Christians who were outside his church's beliefs were also going to hell.

I guess I was naive at the time. I didn't know people like that existed. It was my way or the highway. Soon after that, I checked it out and found that was the foundation of Christianity. *"I am the way, the truth, and the life. No one can come to the Father except through me"* (John 14:6).

It shouldn't be a surprise to anyone that fundamental Christians would embrace this belief. Such statements like this one are sprinkled throughout the Old and New Testament: *"When the Lord Jesus is revealed from heaven with his mighty angels in flaming fire, inflecting vengeance upon those who do not obey the Gospel of our Lord Jesus, they shall suffer the punishment of eternal destruction and exclusion from the presence of the Lord"* (Thessalonians 1:6–9).

This passage urges the killing of people who worship other Gods:

> *If your very own brother, or your son or daughter, or the wife you love, or your closest friend secretly entices you, saying, "Let us go and worship other gods" (gods that neither you nor your fathers have known, gods of the peoples around you, whether near or far, from one end of the land to the other), do not yield to him or listen to him. Show him no pity. Do not spare him or shield him. You must certainly put him to death. Your hand must be the first in putting him to death, and then the hands of all the people. Stone him to death, because he tried to turn you away from the* LORD*...* (Deuteronomy 13:6–10)

> Jesus said, *"If a man abide not in me, he is cast forth as a branch, and is withered: and men gather them, and cast them into fire, and they are burned."* (John 15:6)

Years later, I learned Catholics and some Protestant denominations revised their interpretation of the Scriptures, opening the gates of heaven to a wider audience. Vatican II (1962–'65) declared those who practice other great religions of the world and even those who have no religion at all but strive to live according to the graces that God gave us can be saved. Unfortunately, there are still a great many Christians, including most evangelicals and other fundamentalists, who still hold to the belief that salvation can only be achieved through the acceptance of Christ. Some don't like to admit to the belief because they know it makes them look bad in the eyes of others outside their faith. I think they know it's wrong but can't let go of the belief because they think it would signal a breakdown in their faith. They're no different than some radical Muslims who believe all Christians (infidels) are going to hell because they don't believe their story about Mohammad.

What that fundamental minister said left a lasting impression on me. He represented the dark side of Christianity. There was no way I could ever think God would like anyone telling people of other religions that by not accepting their faith, they're going to hell. It was the most divisive statement about other people and their religions I had ever heard. Like most people, I used to think God was synonymous with religion. I don't think that's true. I believe if there's a god, he's not a Christian, Muslim, Jew, Buddhist, or any other religion devised by man. He's just God. I believe he'll accept people of all faiths and people of no faith. If we're judged, I'd like to believe it'll be based on whether we lived a righteous life rather than our choice of religions. If by chance, heaven is the exclusive domain for evangelicals or some other like-minded group, I'm not sure that's where I want to spend eternity. I've always valued diversity, and those are not my kind of people.

**What about the Right-to-life movement?** I don't know anyone on either side of the political aisle who wants more abortions, yet the Christian right has turned this issue into a moral battleground on what they claim is God's work. It's interesting to note the Bible is silent on abortion. It's one of many implied moral positions taken by the Christian right in order to promote their moral agenda.

Ironically, it could be argued God is the most prolific of all the abortionists. Fifty percent of all human conceptions end up in a spontaneous abortion with women often not even knowing they were pregnant. Twenty percent of all recognized pregnancies end up in miscarriages. It could be argued God is the most prolific of the abortionists.*

---

* Harris, 38. Fifty percent of all human conceptions end up in a spontaneous abortion with woman often not even knowing they were pregnant. Twenty percent of all recognized pregnancies end up in miscarriages. It could be argued God is the most prolific of the abortionists.

Abortions were performed before the Supreme Court made it legal with *Roe v. Wade* in 1973, but they were done illegally in back-alley butcher shops, resulting in countless deaths or women being so badly butchered they were unable to ever bear children. It was mostly the poor who suffered under that system. The wealthy could afford to have the procedure done safely.

Studies show women are just as likely to get abortions in countries where it's legal as they are in countries where it's outlawed, according to the Gilda Sedgh of Guttmacher Institute and the World Health Organizations, published in 2007. Laws don't stop abortions. The same study also reports seventy thousand women die every year from unsafe abortions.* Poverty contributes to abortions more than any other factor. Women who have little or no means to support a child look to abortion as a way to solve their problem.

If the right-to-life movement really wants to reduce abortions, they would join with others to reduce poverty, provide better educational opportunities for the poor, support sex education in our schools, encourage the use of contraceptives and family planning. They would also join with others to provide a safety net for unwed mothers who are poor such as free prenatal care, childcare, and making adoptions an easier option. Without those kinds of actions, abortions will continue to be performed regardless of what happens with *Roe v. Wade*.

I've always been troubled with the right-to-life movement because of their many contradictions. They seem to support the taking of life in other ways.

We're the only industrialized country that still has capital punishment. Most countries view our use of the death penalty as barbaric. When George Bush, the evangelical president, was the governor of Texas, he presided over 152 executions. Texas has long been known as the leader in state executions, and it also claims to be the state with one of the largest populations of evangelical Christians. I

---

* Marcia Cheng, AP Medical Writer, http://www.newsvine.com/_news/2007/ 10/11/1019458legalstatusdoesntdeterabortion, October 11, 2007. Studies show women are just as likely to get an abortion in countries where it's legal as they are in countries where it's outlawed…

seldom hear anyone from the right-to-life movement argue against the death penalty. To add to the dilemma, the use of DNA testing reveals that far too many innocent people have been executed or are on death row for crimes they didn't commit. One reason why evangelicals might be comfortable with the death penalty is that it's the most mentioned punishment in the Bible.

The Christian right seems to be full of contradictions. The preemptive invasion of Iraq is one of them. The Christian right represented President Bush's strongest group of supporters during the invasion even though Iraq had nothing to do with 9/11. The war took the life of thousands of young Americans with many more coming home physically or emotionally disabled. It caused the deaths of well over one hundred thousand Iraqis with millions more being displaced. The cost has been estimated to be in the trillions. We could have used that money for so many better reasons. Most Americans have come to believe it was a war of choice and not of necessity. It was a war that shouldn't have been fought. It's beyond me how anyone could have supported that kind of bloodshed and human suffering while calling themselves a right-to-lifer.

**What about the Christian right and homosexuality?** Their position is that same-sex relationships are against what God believes and that marriage should only be between a man and a woman. The biblical passage they often cite is: "*If a man lies with a man as one lies with a woman, both of them have done what is detestable. They must be put to death; their blood will be on their own heads*" (Leviticus 20:13).

They don't have a lot of scripture they can point to in their defense since the concept of homosexuality and lesbianism leading to a committed long-term relationship was not developed until the twentieth century. Thus one cannot expect to find many biblical references to same-sex marriages. Just like there are no references to planes, trains, or automobiles in the Scriptures. That hasn't prevented the Christian Right from trying to drive gays and lesbians back into their closets.

This is another example of a discriminatory position the Christian Right lost to public opinion and human decency. Many fundamental Christians once claimed it was God who called out gays for their sinful ways. They were just doing God's work. Did God change his mind?

**What about Christian missionary work?** I've always had a strong social conscience, and I remember as a young child being troubled when watching films on television showing Christian missionaries spreading their message about Christ among people whose societies were less advanced. Much of that took place in Africa and South America in the first half of the twentieth century. It bothered me to know they were being enticed with trinkets and modern marvels from the Western world as a trade-off for giving up their heritage, culture, and way of life to accept Christ. Sadly, their conversion was followed by years of colonization by Christian nations, resulting in the exploitation of their land, resources, and people. They were stripped of their dignity and thrust into a world of racism, violence, and poverty. In my opinion, their lives were not made better. At the same time, the world lost forever the lessons we could have learned from their cultures.

I'll concede that today, most missionaries do good work in alleviating human suffering. However, I would respect them more if their only reason for helping others were for humanitarian reasons rather than spreading their faith. I believe charity is best when there's nothing to be gained by the donor except the satisfactions that comes from helping others who are less fortunate.

I've always wondered why fundamental Christians think it's their mission in life to spread their faith. Most people belonging to other religions take a live-and-let-live approach to their religion. Fundamental Christians have a long history of promoting their faith through their missionary work, their political involvement, and even in their personal relationships with others. It often produces a negative image among others outside their faith.

**What about the sexual molestation of children within the Catholic Church?** In 2004, the Catholic Church sanctioned a study documenting sex abuse by their clergy. The study concluded that 4 percent of the clerics had been accused of molesting minors since 1950.* In 2007, the Associated Press reported there were five hun-

---

* "Two Studies Cite Child Sex Abuse by 4% of Priests," n.d. http://select.nytimes.com/gst/abstract.html?res=FB0813FC3A580C748EDDAB0894DC404482&n=Top%2fReference%2fTimes%20Topics%2fOrganizations%2fJ%2fJohn%20Jay%20College%20of%20Criminal%20Justice. Article by Laurie Goodstein

dred clergy abuse cases going back sixty years in the Los Angeles Archdiocese, 552 cases in Boston, and 360 cases in Covington, Kentucky. Five other dioceses had filed for bankruptcy. It's been estimated the number of victims is around eleven thousand. The actual number may never be known since most incidents of sexual abuse go unreported. The total cost to the church will exceed well over two billion dollars. Sadly, this has been an ongoing problem with the Catholic Church for a long time, and it's not just confined to the United States.

The fact that these incidents occurred is sad enough but to add to the sadness is the fact that church leaders (bishops) knew about those abuses and protected the offenders at the expense of thousands in innocent children. It wasn't until the national scandal broke with the arrest of priest John Geoghan in Boston that the full extent of the problem became known. Even then some bishops were slow to admit any wrongdoing.

This scandal may seem like a recent problem within the Catholic Church; however, I remember a few years ago watching a documentary about people who had been placed in Catholic orphanages during the first part of the twentieth century. They had come together years later to talk about the physical, emotional, and sexual abuse they received as children in those orphanages. The official response of the Catholic Church was that those were different times and offered no apologies. Anyone who knows anything about the Catholic Church knows they are slow to admit guilt, often taking centuries to apologize for their wrongdoing.

I believe if a secular organization was found guilty of those kinds of horrific sexual abuse acts against children, the public would demand the institution be disbanded and wouldn't rest until everyone responsible was serving time. That didn't happen. The Catholic Church was allowed to do what it's always done—pay off their victims. We have a long tradition in this country of holding religious institutions to a lower standard of accountability than secular institutions.

---

(NYT); National Desk, Late Edition - Final Section A, Page 1, column 1. (3 March 2004). Sexual molestation of children within the Catholic church.

Since that scandal broke, I've heard a number of Catholic experts say they estimate homosexuals made up 20 to 30 percent of the priesthood. That's not to say homosexuals commit more child abuse crimes than heterosexuals. However, it does explain why most of the sexual abuse was aimed at young boys. Some also say that because of celibacy, the priesthood attracts an unusually high number of men who are sexually maladjusted. That's an understatement. Ironically, the Catholic Church opposes same-sex marriages.

Had the church accepted women up through the highest levels of their organization and allowed priests to marry instead of perpetuating a men's club, I don't believe those scandals would have happened. I believe celibacy will someday be recognized as a curse on the Catholic Church. As a side note, it was in 1015 that church laws forbid priests to marry. It was said to be the law of the church and not of God. It was done to prevent children from inheriting church property.

The purpose for writing about this scandal is not to discredit the many good people in the Catholic Church but to point out where organized religion has strayed and caused irreparable harm. It's something people don't like to associate with religion, but unfortunately, it happens much too often, and it's not confined to the Catholic Church. Sexual scandals among the clergy of all faiths seem to make the news on a regular basis, and I'm sure it happens more than what we know. Frequently the clergy who are accused of the misconduct have a reputation for making strong moral judgments about others who commit the same kinds of acts. Often the people we look to for moral leadership are just as likely to fall victim to the kinds of transgressions they devoted their life preaching against. It's the human condition that makes everyone prone to temptation and sin, but when it happens to spiritual leaders, it's viewed as the worst kind of hypocrisy.

**How has generational influences changed Christianity?** I contend that Christianity and religion in general are not static but are always in a state of flux. I've witnessed that over my lifetime.

When I entered my young adult years in the late '50s and early '60s, most people I knew who were my age didn't attend church even if they came from churchgoing families. When my generation came of age, we saw a world where if religion wasn't promoting injustice, it showed a high tolerance for it. My generation wasn't too far removed from a time when the government and churches turned a blind eye to the Ku Klux Klan of our parents' generation and the vigilantly lynching of Blacks in the Bible Belt. We saw the Jim Crow system firsthand on TV. We came of age during the Civil Rights Movement. The Holocaust was still fresh in everyone's mind, and we witnessed the anti-Semitism of our parents' generation. We saw how religion either played a hand in some of those injustices or how ineffective it was in preventing them. We entered adulthood, leaving behind the religion of our parents' generation. Many predicted a continued decline in the role religion would play in future generations.

That prediction appeared to come true for a while. The generation of young people that soon followed called their movement the counterculture revolution. It grew out of Haight-Ashbury and peaked during Woodstock. It was about drugs, peace, and free love. That generation rebelled against everything that was held sacred by their parents, including religion. The country was torn apart by assassinations, racial violence, and the Vietnam War. It came to a close during the Watergate scandal, leaving the country torn and struggling to find its national identity.

The country was tired of the chaos of the '60s and was eager to return to calmer waters. The mainstream youth of the next generation showed little interest in social reform but instead turned inward. Every generation wants to find something new and different from their parents' generation, and that's when the fundamental, evangelical, Christian right movement took root. Young adults turned to that movement to give meaning to their lives. They abandoned the traditional churches of their grandparents and the nonreligious nature of their parents and thus another movement was born. That generation produced Jerry Falwell and the Moral Majority, Pat Robertson and his Christian Coalition, and the rebirth of Evangelicalism. They took a strong stand against abortion, fought to reinstate school prayer, rejected gays, fought to end stem cell research, and denied evolution in support of the biblical story of creation. Their religious beliefs became as fundamental as any time in our country's history. Their influence even carried over to politics as a major player in setting the agenda within the Republican Party.

Today I think the movement's matured and is losing its appeal. Mainstream America is ready for another change. Many fundamental Christians are even becoming disillusioned with the movement. The pendulum is once again swinging.

The point I'm making is that much of how people view religion has a lot to do with when they came of age. Religious beliefs usually take root and shape our lives as we enter our young adult years. That's why my beliefs about religion are not in sync with the generation of my parents or that of my children's generation. They're unique to my age and time. Collectively, those movements have shaped our national character for both good and bad.

*Conclusion*

Some people might think it's unfair to blame Christianity for all the issues I raised in this chapter. My goal was to confront the many myths perpetuated by the Christian right and other fundamental Christian groups. It represents the truth as I discovered it.

# A Source of Unity or Conflict?

*Intolerance comes when people confuse faith with facts. Religious beliefs are based on faith or hope that something is true. There's nothing wrong with faith so long as it's taken for what it is. We all have faith in something. It's when people begin to think faith beliefs are indisputable facts that religious fanaticism and extremism raises its ugly head.*

—Al Vercellino

*Religion is an insult to human dignity. With or without it, you'd have good people doing good things and evil people doing bad things, but for good people to do bad things, it takes religion.*

—Steven Weinberg, Nobel Laureate in Physics

It sometimes raises eyebrows among my Christian friends when I say organized religions have done as much harm as good in the world. I came to that conclusion by viewing organized religions in broad historical terms rather than from a personal perspective of local churches. While many churches and religious organizations do good work, there's always been serious conflicts in the world, resulting in needles deaths and human suffering with religion playing a major role in those conflicts.

From a broad historical perspective, organized religions have probably been as much at fault for causing pain and suffering as other causes such as conflicts over territory, resources, revenge, power, and ideology. Even when religion isn't the main cause, it's often a contributing factor.

Religion often takes on the characteristic of tribalism. We see Jews siding with other Jews, Muslims siding with Muslims, Evangelicals with Evangelicals, and Catholics with Catholics. More often than not that kind of group identity serves to divide rather than unite and is antithetical to the concept of "one human family" that I favor.

Religious conflicts have played a major role in world events during my lifetime. I was born at the beginning of World War II, when six million Jews were being persecuted. During most of my life, Catholics and Protestants were killing each other in Northern Ireland. The ethnically rooted war in Bosnia and Herzegovina between Serbs, Muslims, and Croats resulted in tens of thousands of needles deaths. The Middle East has always been a hotbed of religious strife. It began as a conflict between Israel and its Arab neighbors and expanded to include conflicts between Jews, Christians, and Muslims and later between Sunni and Shiite Muslims.

Even though there's usually multiple causes for world conflicts, few would disagree that religious differences often fuel the flames and make them worse. From the birth of Christ to the present day, there's never been a time when religious differences weren't playing a major role in human suffering.

*Early religious conflicts*

*Persecution of Christians:* When Christianity was evolving as a new religion, Christians were persecuted by the Romans. While that lasted a few hundred years, it was pale compared to how Christianity treated others when they became a dominate force in the world.

*The Crusades:* The Crusades (1095–1291) became the first major religious conflict in the world. It was about Christians and Muslims killing each other for control of the holy lands. Some historians say the period lasted for five hundred years since there was never a clear winner.

Contrary to popular belief, the purpose of the Crusades was not to convert Muslims to Christianity. By the eighth century, Muslim armies had conquered Asia Minor (modern Turkey) and the holy lands, which had been Christian since the time of St. Paul. In desperation, the emperor of Constantinople sent word to the Christians of Western Europe asking for help. That gave birth to the Crusades. It was a response to more than four centuries of conquests in which Muslims had already captured two-thirds of the Christian world. Christianity as a faith and a culture had no choice but to defend itself or be over taken by Islam.

The two goals of the Crusades were to rescue the Christians of the East and to liberate Jerusalem and other locations made holy by the life of Christ. Crusaders saw themselves as pilgrims. From their perspective, Muslims were the enemies of Christ and his church. Some argue that jihad and the strong feelings some Muslims have against the Western world today have their roots in the Crusades.

In the eyes of some Crusaders, Jews like Muslims were also the enemies of Christ.

*The Inquisition:* After the Crusades, the church turned its sights inward, combating heresy and witchcraft. The papal Inquisition started in 1352 and functioned most widely in Northern Italy and Southern France. The Spanish Inquisition started in 1478 and was introduced into the colonies of Mexico, Peru, Sicily, and the Netherlands. It wasn't suppressed in Spain until the early nineteenth century. It even raised its ugly head for a short time among Puritan settlers in New England.

During the Inquisition, suspected heretics were arrested, interrogated, and tried. The use of torture was common. Penalties ranged from prayer and fasting to imprisonment. Convicted heretics who refused to recant were often executed. Many of the victims were Jews and Moors. There are no official records of how many people were killed or tortured during the Inquisition; however, no one would disagree that the Inquisition represented one of Christianity's deepest slides into the depths of intolerance.

The Catholic Church wasn't alone in spreading hatred. Martin Luther and John Calvin, the two Protestant founders, also advocated the wholesale murder of heretics, apostates, Jews, and witches.*

---

* Harris, 12. Martin Luther and John Calvin, the two Protestant founders, advocated the wholesale murder of heretics, apostates, Jews and witches.

*The Jewish issue:* A summary of historical religious conflicts and intolerance wouldn't be complete without saying something about the two thousand years of Jewish persecution by Christians. It's common knowledge the Christian Church taught that Jews (past, present, and future) were responsible for the death of Jesus.* The Gospels (particularly the gospel of John) contains many passages condemning the Jews as sons of Satan and accusing them of murdering Jesus (John 8:42–44). The church also believed that some Jews must be allowed to live because the biblical book of Revelation claimed they had a role to play in the "end-time." They concluded it was acceptable to persecute Jews, and they did that in almost every decade during the two thousand years of Christianity. It led to the extermination of Jews throughout the Christian movement up through modern times. It's a sad, long, and brutal act of genocide that in its entirety equals anything in the history of civilization. It's no wonder that today there are only fourteen million Jews in the world representing only .2 percent of the world's population while there are 1.9 billion Christians. Sadly, most Christians aren't aware of their history of persecuting Jews, and not surprisingly, it's something most church leaders don't like to talk about.

A complete review of the two thousand years of Christianity's attempts at Jewish extermination would be too lengthy to list, so I'll just highlight some of the more significant events below:*

- *1205:* Pope Innocent III wrote to the archbishops of Sens and Paris that "the Jews, by their own guilt, are consigned to perpetual servitude because they crucified the Lord..."
- *1215:* The Fourth Lateran Council approved cannon laws requiring Jews and Muslims to wear special dress so they

---

* "Anti-Semitism and Anti-Judaism within the Roman Catholic Church 1st to 20th Century CE," n.d. http://www.religioustolerance.org/vat_hol11.htm (12 December 2004). Jews being blamed for Jesus' death.

* "A Overview of 2000 Years of Jewish Persecution Anti-Judaism: 1201 1800 CE," n.d. Ontario Consultants on Religious Tolerance, n.d. http://www. religioustolerance.org/jud_pers3.htm (January 5, 2005). Jewish persecution of Jews. This site contains a more comprehensive list of Jewish persecution than contained in this book.

could be distinguished from Christians. This practice spread to other countries.

- *1227:* The Synod of Narbonne required Jews to wear an oval badge. This practice was later adopted by Hitler, who replaced the oval badge with the Star of David.
- *1229:* Pope Innocent IV authorized the use of torture while Duke Henry III of Belgium announced Jews must be expelled and totally annihilated until there are no Jews.
- *1298:* More than one hundred thousand Jews were killed over a six-month period in Austria, Bavaria, and Franconia.
- *1306:* One hundred thousand Jews were exiled from France. They left with only the clothes on their backs and food for one day.
- *1321:* Five thousand Jews were burned alive at the stake for being accused of having incited criminals to poison wells in Guienne, France.
- *1347-plus:* Twenty-five million people died during the plague. People looked for someone to blame, and since a smaller percentage of Jews caught the disease, they blamed the Jews. Their smaller numbers were probably due to the Jewish sanitary and dietary laws they preserved from the Old Testament. Rumors spread that Satan was protecting the Jews because the devil was paying them back for poisoning wells used by Christians. Some historians estimate it led to the murder of more than twenty-five thousand Jews throughout Europe.
- *1354:* Twelve thousand Jews were executed in Toledo.
- *1492:* Three hundred thousand Jews left Spain penniless when given the choice of being baptized or banished.
- *1516:* The first ghetto was formed in Europe when the governor of the Republic of Venice decided Jews would be permitted to live in one area of the city. Hitler made use of this concept in the 1930s.
- *1648–9:* One hundred thousand Jews were murdered and three hundred communities were destroyed in the Ukraine.
- *1873:* Wilhelm Marr coined the term "anti-Semitism" in a pamphlet called "Jewry's Victory over Teutonism."

- *1915:* One hundred thousand Jews died of exposure or starvation when six hundred thousand Jews were forcibly moved from the western borders of Russia toward the interior.*

Some people believe all the acts committed against Jews were the fault of evil leaders. That may be true to a point, but those acts wouldn't have been possible without the widespread belief by Christians that Jews were responsible for the death of Jesus. It gave them the excuse to use Jews as scapegoats. It's also unfair to blame God. It's the fault of people and their misguided use of religion.

*Nazi Germany and the Jews:* The extermination of six million Jews during WWII is still fresh in our memories. Almost everyone accepts the horror of that event and conveniently place all the blame on Adolf Hitler. That to me is too simplistic and doesn't tell the whole story.

Hitler wrote in Mein Kemp, *"Today I believe that I am acting in accordance with the will of the Almighty Creator by defending myself against the Jews."* He was playing to the anti-Semitic feelings among Christians that existed in Germany and around the world during the time of his rise to power. At that time, anti-Semitism was widespread in Greece, Hungary, Mexico, Poland, Romania, and the USSR. Even in the United States, there were supporters of Hitler's hatred of Jews. Radio programs by many conservative American clergy, both Roman Catholic and Protestant, frequently attacked Jews. Father Caughlin, Henry Ford, Charles Lindbergh, Joseph Kennedy, and many other prominent Americans were sympathetic to Hitler's hatred of Jews. Hitler played on that hatred to rally his countrymen to place Jews in concentration camps, eventually exterminating six million while the rest of the world stood by. While not to excuse Hitler, it was the German people consisting mostly of Catholics and Lutherans who also need to take responsibility for what happened in those death camps. Furthermore, I believe the entire world has to take responsibility for turning its backs on the plight of the Jews during that dark period in our history.

---

* Ibid. (Anti-Semitism: Racially-based persecution of Jews 1800 to 1946). Jewish persecution of Jews. This site contains a more comprehensive list of Jewish persecution than contained in this book.

The role of Christian churches during the Holocaust can be described as silent or indifferent. Even after the Holocaust was known the Catholic Church's official position under Pope Pius XII was that of neutrality toward Nazi Germany. The Lutheran Church, which was the largest Protestant denomination in Germany, fared no better. Martin Luther, the founder of the church, made no secret of his hatred for Jews. Both churches had a long history of anti-Semitism. It can be argued that had they come out against the Nazis, their survival would have been threatened. That's a matter of conscience that history will have to decide.

It took the Roman Catholic Church until 1966 to declare that all present-day Jews can't be blamed for the death of Jesus. It's hard to believe it took the church more than two decades after the slaughter of six million Jews to lift the curse they placed on them for two thousand years.

While the hatred of Jews by Christians stemmed from the belief they were responsible for Jesus's death, I'm sure by the mid-twentieth century, that reason didn't motivate most of the hatred toward Jews in this country. I believe it was mostly stereotyping and hatred being passed down from one generation to another. I remember as a young child growing up around Detroit (1940s and early '50s), my parents and most of their Christian friends didn't like Jews. They never mentioned anything about Jews being responsible for the death of Jesus. They just didn't like Jews. For example, if anyone pulled out in front of my dad driving an expensive car, he'd call him a "damn Jew." To illustrate how prevalent anti-Semitism was in this country even after the Holocaust, I'm reminded of reading about Bess Truman never allowing Jews in their home in Independence, Missouri. Ironically, it was President Truman who went against public opinion to recognize Israel. The United States has a checkered history when it comes to anti-Semitism.

Most people label Hitler an atheist. The fact is he was raised a Catholic and attended Catholic schools. There's no evidence he ever renounced his faith.* It can be argued his anti-Semitism grew out of his Christian education. Christian Austria and Germany during his

---

* Dawkins, 273–274, Hitler was raised a Catholic and attended Catholic schools. There's no evidence he ever renounced his faith.

time took for granted the belief that Jews held an inferior status to Aryan Christians. The hatred didn't originate from Hitler; it came from the preaching of Catholic priests and Protestant leaders. Some say it was less about his personal feelings and more about playing to the anti-Semitism that existed in Germany at the time. Whatever his motivation, he was a master at demagoguery, and the Jews made a convenient scapegoat for Germany's past failures.

Whatever Hitler believed, we can't blame it on atheism. People of religion like to perpetuate the myth that atheists are responsible for all the evils in the world while denying the role religion has played in human suffering. I won't deny that some people who claim to be an atheist sometimes commit evil acts, but it's usually not in the name of atheism. They're just evil people. Stalin is a good example. He did terrible things to people because of his evil nature. He didn't use atheism as the reason. When religious people commit evil acts, they usually do it in the name of religion. I can't think of one evil historical event that was done in the name of atheism, but I can cite a never-ending list of evil acts committed in the name of religion.

Steven Weinberg, a Nobel Laureate in physics, once said, *"Religion is an insult to human dignity. With or without it, you's have good people doing good things and evil people doing bad things, but for good people to do bad things, it takes religion."*

Not all Christians can be blamed for the two thousand years of Jewish persecution or the Holocaust. There were Christians who came to the defense of the Jews. Their stories are well chronicled. Unfortunately, they weren't a large-enough group nor influential enough to change the course of history.

*What does it mean today?*

I'm sure many Christians today would ask, What does two thousand years of Jewish persecution by Christians and the Holocaust have to do with me and my church? I wasn't around then. My church didn't exist when that happened. Some might even say those people who persecuted Jews weren't Christians, but they were the Christians of their time just like the Christians who supported slavery before the Civil War, the Christians who supported Jim Crow laws after the Civil War, the Christians who opposed civil rights for Blacks in the '50s and '60s, and the Christians who opposed gay and lesbian unions. They were Christians on the wrong side of history. It seems to me most Christians live in denial when it comes to dealing with the reality of what Christianity has done to people outside their faith or people who are different.

Even today, the Bible continues to drive the thinking of fundamental Christians in their attitudes about Jews and others outside their faith. In the book of Revelation, it describes the Rapture, which prophesies that during the end-time, Christ will raise those who believe in him to be with God and leave all others including Jews who choose not to be converted to suffer during Armageddon. For that to happen, Jews have to be occupying Palestine. That's one of the reasons we see so many fundamental Christian groups supporting Israel. The belief in this medieval myth by a significant number of fundamental Christians undermines our effort to achieve mutual respect and trust between Christians, Muslims, and Jews.

Perhaps our biggest mistake was to invade and occupy Muslim countries (Afghanistan and Iraq) while ignoring the religious differences and mutual distrust that exists between our cultures. We destroyed Iraq and caused the death and displacement of tens of thousands of innocent people while fueling the flames of jihad in a way that hasn't happened since the Crusades. That and the fact that our addiction to oil has caused us to support repressive regimes in the region while overlooking their lack of commitment to human rights. While looking after our self-interest, we've often failed to win over the hearts and minds of the Muslim people.

We sometimes display a superior attitude toward other people and countries as if we are the center of the universe and all other nations are subordinate. This attitude is easy to advance because of our wealth, military might, and being the only superpower. If history is right, that won't last forever.

The attitude of superiority often carries over to religion. We sometimes give the impression that Christianity is superior to other religions and act as if people who embrace other religions aren't right with God. The fact is the majority of the people in the world are not Christians. Islam (Muslims) is growing faster than Christianity and is predicted to become the largest religion in the world. That's happening at an accelerated pace in most of Europe. In time, Europe could become inhabited by more Muslims than Christians. It seems to me it would be in our best interest to give up our holier-than-thou attitude about being a Christian nation and begin embracing a world in which religious diversity is a fact of life.

To give the reader a better understanding of the religious diversity in the world, I've included a chart showing the breakdown of the world's religions.

*Religious Breakdown by Population (2000):*[*]

- 33 percent Christians
- 19.6 percent Muslims
- 13.4 percent Hindus
- 12.7 percent nonreligious
- 6.4 percent Chinese Folk
- 5.9 percent Buddhists
- 3.8 percent ethnoreligionists
- 2.5 percent atheists
- 1.7 percent new religionists
- .4 percent Sikhs
- .4 percent others
- .2 percent Jews

*Conclusion*

It would be nice if all religions would do more to unite us rather than divide and serve as our conscience to help us do what's right. We know that hasn't been the case. At best, religions mirror society with

---

[*] "Religions of the World: Numbers of Adherents; names of houses of worship; names of leaders; rates of growth…," n.d., http://www.religioustolerance.org/rel_rate.htm (2 February 2004). Religious Breakdown by Population - 2000

all its virtues, flaws, and imperfections. At worst, it leads us to dark places time has made us regret.

It sometimes scares me to think that had I been a Christian anytime in history, the odds are that I would have identified with one of those movements that brought about pain and suffering in the world in behalf of God and religion.

I didn't cover all the religious conflicts throughout history since it would take volumes. Hopefully, what I covered helped make my point that organized religions with its intolerance for others who hold different beliefs have caused great pain and suffering in the world. I'll leave it up to the reader to decide whether organized religions have created more harm than good.

# What It All Means

*Some people may think I'm going to hell for my views about God and religion. They'd probably find it hard to believe that I hold the opposite view. I have faith that if there is a God, he'll thank me for trying to set the record straight. I think he'll agree with me that he's been poorly served by people and their religions throughout history. I know he won't fault me for attempting to seek the truth. If there is no God, my message is even more important.*

*—Al Vercellino*

As you might have guessed, I found Christianity and other organized religions not believable with far too many trappings for me to embrace. I'm sure I'm not alone in arriving at that conclusion. We all have to find our own way. Even within the Christian faith, few people see it the same way.

I concluded there's a difference between being religious and being spiritual. Some of the nicest people I've met probably believed in God but were not religious. They projected inner peace, love, compassion, and kindness. They were innately good and a joy to be around. They lived their lives in harmony with the spirit of Christianity more than many Christians I've known. At the same time, I've met devoutly religious people who seemed devoid of those qualities.

## Morality

I'm often confronted with the notion that I must be morally inferior to those who claim religious affiliation. It's not socially acceptable to openly reject Christianity. The same is true in Arab countries for people who reject Islam. To suggest that, in my opinion, Christianity is fraught with problems or that Christians have committed terrible acts against humanity invites the perception that I must not be a good person.

I'm bothered when Christians think I have to yield the moral high ground to them. One of the reasons I rejected church affiliation and organized religion is because I didn't think it would make me a better person. Furthermore, I just couldn't embrace their belief system. That doesn't make me a morally inferior person. As I said earlier, during my life, I've observed that Christians in general were no more inclined to do the right thing in terms of being morally or ethically right than non-Christians. As I've already pointed out, I believe Christianity has been on the wrong side of too many human rights and social issues for me to embrace.

My claim about how people feel about the morals of those who have no religious affiliation is not without some basis. That answer varies by country. In a poll conducted by the Pew Research Center's Global Attitudes Project, it asked if people had to believe in God to be moral. Here are the results: 89 percent of the Pakistanis, 58 percent of Americans, 25 percent of the Britons, and only 13 percent of the French said it is necessary to believe in God to be moral. In many ways, when it comes to religious fundamentalism, Americans are often viewed as being on the extreme end of the continuum.

Some people may wonder how it's possible to have a strong value system and morals without religious beliefs. I would first say it's probably not easy for anyone to develop a strong value system. It's a lifetime pursuit. As I said at the beginning of this book, I found all the major religions promoted the same basic messages about how we should live our lives. They're often referred to as natural laws. I looked at religious values and took a Buddhist saying, "From good comes good and from evil comes evil," which I thought encompassed everything from all the religions and could be applied to how I would choose to live my life. While this statement seemed simple, I thought it profound. I didn't think I needed an ancient text to help me decide good and evil or right from wrong. In my opinion, any sane person has that capacity. The challenge is to practice good over evil. I felt this simple rule placed me in harmony with the "good" in most of the religions. The meaning of this statement is not unlike the golden rule: "Do unto others as you would like done unto you." It's interesting to point out that some version of the golden rule can be found in all the major religions. I take some comfort in knowing if there is a God and he judges me, he'll say while I was far from perfect, I tried to do the right thing most of the time. I think the best thing that can be said about anyone in their journey through life is that they tried to leave the world a better place than they found it. That doesn't have to be in a world-altering way but in the way we relate with others as we go about our daily lives. One measure of this is whether we gave more than we took.

I also discovered determining right from wrong is not always as easy as it sounds. We're sometimes confronted with complex social issues or situations that are more gray than black or white. They don't always lend themselves to simple right or wrong answers. To make those decisions, it's not likely that I would look to ancient writings that have their roots in mythology. I rely on history, cultural and political influences, the social sciences, and respected scholars and journalists. Lastly I apply rational thinking, common sense, and follow my conscience. That doesn't mean I'm always right. It's my hope that when my mind is made up that I'm open to opposing viewpoints and willing to adjust my beliefs based on new information. In my opinion, that's something organized religions and their followers have difficulty doing. Too often they're stuck in long-held archaic beliefs or church dogma and are extremely slow to change their minds. They tend to see the world in absolute arbitrary truths while I find very few absolute truths in my life.

Whether a person is a member of a religion or is an atheist doing the right thing is probably the most difficult personal challenge we all face. It's not always the most popular thing to do. It can demand courage, personal sacrifice, and rejection. I think for most people, and even nations, it represents the most frequent failing in our journey through life.

*Doubt*

Regardless of what anyone believes, I think there's always some doubt. Death is an unsolved mystery regardless of one's faith. No one can prove God exists or doesn't exist. The search is part of everyone's journey. We're all guessing, hoping, and speculating about why we're here and what happens after we die.

Doubt might explain why almost everyone seems to fear death. Even the most devout believers pray to God to keep them and their loved ones alive. If heaven exists, they don't seem too eager get there. Regardless of one's beliefs, most people show the same sadness and grief when a loved one dies. Even among the faithful death is often a scary thing.

If Christians really have unquestioned faith in an afterlife, I wonder why they don't ask people who are near death to take messages to loved ones when they pass over to the other side? I've never known that to happen even though it's a common practice when people leave on a long trip to visit friends and relatives here on earth.

*Choices*

I've always been puzzled why some people are drawn to organized religion while others aren't. It seems to me it has something to do with their mental makeup or personality. Many of the most fervent believers I've known have been people who didn't grow up with a strong religious upbringing. They gravitated in that direction later in life. Why do some people see religion as playing no role or a small role in their lives while others immerse themselves in religion in a way that defines and dominates who they are?

In my case, I'm fiercely independent and self-reliant. Surrendering independent thinking to "group think" would be difficult for me. I don't have the mental makeup or personality for that kind of submission. If there is a God, I believe he gave us the ability to think for ourselves.

Because I take pride in thinking for myself, I've always been weary of anyone who claims to have all the answers to the meaning of life and what happens after we die based on what they've been taught in church. That doesn't mean I deny the existence of God, nor does it mean I accept his existence. I just don't know.

Polls show 85 percent to 95 percent of Americans say they believe in God. That belief is not confined to the Christian God. There are a lot of reasons for that belief. We're often drawn to God when we face hardships and tragedies. Like I said earlier, when people need explanations about events they can't control or understand, they turn to God and religion. That seems to be true when we deal with a serious illness or the death of loved ones or when we have to deal with our own death. Most people don't want to believe death is final. They take comfort in believing they'll be united with loved ones. For many, life has dealt them a bad hand, and in their struggles, they want to believe there will be a better place for them in another life. Some need religion to guide them in their daily lives to help them decide right from wrong. For many, they feel there needs to be a reward after death for living a good and righteous life. Some even have a need to believe there will be punishment for those who commit evil acts. Others conclude that when everything else fails, all that's left is God and religion to fill their emptiness and provide them with unconditional love. Others just need to believe what they were taught to believe. For many, it's for all the above reasons. They're all reasons to believe in a higher power and embrace religion.

Another argument for believing in God is to look at the wonder of life and the universe and ask how it could have been created without God. It's probably the most powerful argument for the existence of God, but it doesn't make it true.

I've observed that many fundamental evangelical Christians whose lives are dominated by Jesus have unresolved issues and need the unconditional love that can only come from God. That often becomes the driving force that moves some people to make Jesus the center of their life. Many turn to Jesus even before knowing much about the Bible. It's a familiar pattern among many "born-again" Christians.

I've encountered a number of people whose faith is questionable but claim to be a Christian because they would rather be safe than sorry if the promise made by Christianity proves to be true. Some make their move to Christianity as they get older and begin contemplating their own mortality. They're motivated more by fear than their love for Jesus.

It's been reported that the belief in God might be in our genes. Based on mankind's long history of believing in God, there might be some truth to that claim. It has primitive origins. It could also explain why some people find it easy to make the leap of faith while others find it extremely difficult or even impossible. We could be hardwired to believe life is eternal as opposed to death being the end of life.

*Faith versus science*

The role God and religion plays in our lives has changed over time. When we were an agrarian society, our physical and economic well-being depended on the weather and other forces of nature that were not within our control. There was a greater reliance on God and religion in our daily lives since we knew so little about our world. Since the industrial revolution and the information age, we're more dependent on science, medicine, technology, the economy, and society for our well-being. We have greater control over our destiny and less of a need to depend on God and religion.

Many people find the religious answers they once accepted as the truth contradicts much of what we know today. For example, our explorations into space bring us closer every day to explaining the creation of the universe. We know that with the existence of a combination of elements in the right environment, life can spontaneously occur and over time (billions of years) higher life can form (natural selection and evolution). Carbon dating can help us determine the age of our early ancestors. With our understanding of the human genome system, we've been able to trace the origins of our species to Central Africa (that should shock white supremacists). We can now trace our living ancestors as far back as 3.5 million years. We can say with certainty that the genetic makeup of chimpanzees is 97 percent identical to ours.

Everyone knows the church can be slow to accept scientific explanations. An example of how slow the church can be is illustrated in the announcement made by the Catholic Church in 1991 that it was wrong in convicting Galileo in 1616 for challenging the biblical view that the earth was the center of our solar system.

To further illustrate the paradox that often exists between science and religion, I'm reminded of two articles I read on the same day on September 7, 2002. One article was about Rosh Hashana, which Jews believed was the day God created man 5,763 years ago. The other article was about the discovery of a six to seven million-year-old skull that had been unearthed in Central Africa and is expected to change scientific thought about our human origins.

With all that science can tell us, it's within the realm of possibility that someday all the mysteries of life will be unlocked. We may soon have an uncontested explanation of how the universe was formed and how life on our planet originated. We're close to having the power to create life along with the capacity to destroy our planet. When everything is finally known, much of what's contained in ancient religious texts will be much less believable.

*Creation versus evolution*

Most creation supporters don't realize the creation stories in the Bible came from ancient folklore in Egypt and Mesopotamia and didn't originate with the ancient Israelites.

While polls show most Americans believe in the creation story, they seemingly know little about them. For example, many people don't know the Bible offers two accounts of creation. Genesis 1 claims God created the earth in six days and rested on the seventh while Genesis 2 says nothing about it. Genesis 2 describes Adam and Eve and the forbidden fruit while Genesis 1 is silent on the subject. Genesis 1 says God created man first, and Genesis 2 claims he created animals, trees, and plants first. Genesis 1 says he created man before women, and Genesis 2 says he created them at the same time. If that's not confusing, I don't know what is.

The creation stories come with other problems. In Genesis 1 it says God created light on the first day but waited until the fourth day to create the sun, moon, and stars. So where did light come from those first few days? If Adam and Eve were the first people placed on earth (according to Genesis 2), where did Kane, their son, find a wife?

Creation supporters claim the earth was created six thousand years ago while ignoring the fact that there are fossilized human footprints dating back 117,000 years.

Creation believers deny the long-established undisputed scientific facts of natural selection and evolution, which simply states that life adapts to changes in the environment and cites millions of examples where that occurred.

This debate proves once again that religion seems to be the only area in people's lives where ignorance is praised and often considered a virtue.

*Speculations*

I don't think speculation about questions that have vexed humankind since the beginning of time should be discouraged. If anything, the discussion should be encouraged. People of faith often dismiss or ostracize those who suggest other answers to questions they think their faith answers.

There are a variety of answers to the mysteries of life other than Christianity's explanations. I don't think it's beyond the realm of possibility that, like all other life-forms, we live and die. That's it. Even if there is a creator, it could be our fate to have only one life. We accept death to be final with all other life-forms. Like other life-forms, it's possible we're here for no other reason than to propagate our species. We give birth, raise our offspring, and die.

All we really know for sure is that we have one life. Regardless of what happens when we die, life is precious. We owe it to ourselves and others to make it count for something.

While all the Christian denominations I know about believe other life-forms have only one life, I find it odd that at least one of the thirty-four thousand Christian denominations hasn't thought to include pets as having a soul. I know in my case I would be overjoyed if I thought I could spend eternity with all the pets I've been with during my life. For me, it would be better than spending eternity with some of the people I've encountered. This is just another one of my fantasies.

It could be that we return to earth reincarnated, which is the belief of Buddhists and Hindus. That means we could return in different life-forms. That's not something most Christians want to believe, but it can't be excluded from the list of possibilities. It's a belief held by a significant number of people around the world. I for one think there's some merit to the concept. Strange as it may seem, I've met a number of people who call themselves Christians who claim to believe in reincarnation.

It's possible when we have all the answers to the mysteries of life, we'll conclude there is no god. That's a minority view, but it's within the realm of possibility. There are atheists who make a strong argument supporting that claim, and their numbers are growing. The vast majority of the members of the National Academy of Science support that position.

I'm not bothered by not having all the answers. A little mystery in life can be a good thing. It motivates people to keep searching. I've come to realize the supermarket approach offered by all the religions only reinforces my belief that some of the deepest questions in life are as much a mystery today as they've ever been. For me, it's more important that I continue to consider all the possibilities, keep an open mind, and remain curious.

No one has the answer to what happens after we die. It's still as much of a mystery as it's ever been. In my case, I know more about what I don't believe than what I believe.

## Mythology?

Any rational person should be able to distinguish truth from mythology. For example, I have a problem accepting the stories of creation in the book of Genesis as factual. In my opinion, it's nothing more than mythology. If anyone has ever seen the layers of ancient life embedded in rock formations that are billions of years old or held a fossil containing organisms that no longer inhabit the earth, viewed dinosaur bones in a museum, or just marveled at the great diversity in nature, they'd have to acknowledge evolution is real and that all life was not created by God in one fell swoop.

I also have difficulty with the belief that God spoke to someone in ancient times and revealed "the truth" to them. It seems to me if God had something to say to all mankind, he would say it to the entire world, leaving no doubt that he was here and what he said. It defies logic that he would speak to a few chosen people in ancient times while leaving the rest of humanity to accept their word about what he said.

To claim that a baby came from the womb of a teenage girl who claimed to be a virgin and was later declared the son of God, or for that matter God himself, and then died for all our sins has to be the most far-fetched claim ever made by any religion.

There are other claims in the Bible that defy logic, such as a talking snake, donkey, and bush; people living for nine hundred years; a man-made ark containing one pair of all the animals on the planet; being raised from the dead; the Nile turning to blood; food raining from the sky for forty years; witches, wizards, and sorcerers; Moses and his magic wand; Jesus walking on water; angels breaking people out of jail; people healed by Peter's shadow; the story about the "end-time" and the Rapture; a fiery lake of eternal torment awaiting unbelievers under the earth, etc. The list goes on and on.

Today, if someone were to make those claims, their sanity would be seriously questioned. Yet for many Christians, they're considered to be the absolute truth even though they were made two thousand to three thousand years ago in a world where people embraced mythology and believed the earth was flat and the center of the universe.

Christianity is not alone in embracing myths. All religions contain what others outside their faith label as myths. For me, they're no more believable than the stories in the Quran and other religious books. Most religions require us to put aside rational thinking, common sense, and logic in order to embrace their faith.

*Christian theology*

Much has been written about the immoral, unjust, and cruel acts contained in Christian theology.

Christian theology describes God as loving while also being jealous, vindictive, and hateful. If there is a God, he has to be personally offended about the way Christianity has portrayed him. One of the most famous examples is God telling Abraham to sacrifice his only son, Isaac, as a burnt offering to test whether he feared him (Genesis 22:1–12). Other passages about the Christian God are just as horrifying:

> He drowned the entire population of the planet, saving one family. He sent the plague to kill all first born children in Egypt, human and animal. He rained fire and brimstone on Sodom, killing everyone—boys, girls, babies, pregnant women, animals. He sent his Israelite warriors to destroy the neighboring pagan tribes, man, woman, and children.*

If we were describing a mortal being, he would be one of the most evil persons who ever lived.

Because Adam and Eve didn't obey God, Christianity tells us we're all born with original sin, including all newborn babies. The Bible says that's the reason for all the suffering in the world. By today's moral standards, it would be wrong to expect innocent people to take responsibility for the wrongdoings of others. It's not a belief or practice that modern societies embrace in their moral codes or laws.

There are numerous passages throughout the Bible supporting slavery, the subjugation of women, self-castration, human and animal sacrifices, and all kinds of other violent acts.

---

* Barker, 333. "He drowned the entire population of the planet, saving one family. He sent the plague to kill all first born children in Egypt, human and animal. He rained fire and brimstone on Sodom, killing everyone—boys, girls, babies, pregnant women, animals. He sent his Israelite warriors to destroy the neighboring pagan tribes, man, woman, and child."

The New Testament is no better; it gave us hell and eternal damnation to those who don't accept Jesus as their personal savior. Jesus is quoted as saying, *"If a man abide not in me, he is cast forth as a branch, and is withered: and men gather them, and cast them into fire, and they are burned"* (John 15:6). This passage led to the church's execution, with fire, of witches and heretics during the Middle Ages.

The Bible is peppered with passages most fundamental Christians wouldn't allow their children to read. For example: *"Behold, I will corrupt your seed and spread dung upon your faces, even the dung of your solemn feats"* (Malachi 2:3). *"Therefore the Lord will smite with a scab the crown of the head of the daughters of Zion, and the Lord will discover (lay bare) their secret parts (that being the vagina)"* (Isaiah 3:17).

It could be argued there's as much wickedness as there is goodness in the Bible.

*The Ten Commandments*

Much has been said and written about the Ten Commandments being the bedrock of Christian morality and values. Yet few people can recall more than two or three commandments. Here they are:

1. *You shall have no other gods before me.*
2. *You shall not make for yourself a graven image.*
3. *You shall not take the name of the LORD your GOD in vain.*
4. *Remember the Sabbath day, to keep it holy.*
5. *Honor your father and mother.*
6. *You shall not murder.*
7. *You shall not commit adultery.*
8. *You shall not steal.*
9. *You shall not bear false witness against your neighbor.*
10. *You shall not covet your neighbor's house; you shall not covet your neighbor's wife, or his manservant, or his maidservant, or his ox, or his ass, or anything that is your neighbor's.*

The first four commandments have nothing to do with morality. They're statements that Christians have either reinterpreted or ignored. The least controversial is the first one: "*You shall have no other gods before me*," but even that can be challenged. Christianity added Jesus and the trinity to the no other gods before me. Graven images are seen throughout the Christian community. We see them in the form of crucifixes, crosses, statues, paintings, and jewelry. Using the Lord's name in vain is so common most people give it little thought. "*Remember the Sabbath day, to keep it holy*" should be pretty straightforward, but when God gave Moses the Ten Commandments, the Sabbath was celebrated on Saturdays and not Sundays. I think most people would agree the first four commandments have little to do with making the world a better place.

The last six are moral statements but, on close examination, few would label them as earth-shattering proclamations. Any list of rules promoting the moral stability of a social unit would probably contain those statements and more. The last one seems to be ignored the most. As Americans, we covet all the time. Most of our discretionary spending revolves around coveting what our neighbors have. It's what drives our economy. Committing adultery is another commandment that's often ignored by a good many Christians.

The Ten Commandments as we know them don't represent all the commandments in the Old Testament. Many of those that were left out would be an insult to civilized society. We can thank God Christians don't embrace the entire list.

I believe moral values are important. I just don't understand why Christianity holds the Ten Commandments in such high esteem. If they came from God, it certainly wasn't during one of his more lucid or profound moments. I would place a higher value on the Constitution and the Bill of Rights as a foundation for governing a just society even though there's no mention of God.

*Forgiveness and judgment*

All the major religions except Christianity holds each of us responsible for our sins. Christianity is the only religion that gives people a free pass to salvation by merely accepting Christ as their savior. I don't understand how believing that someone else was tortured and died for our sins can make us a better person. That kind of belief takes us off the hook for taking responsibility for our actions and is contrary to the qualities that define mature adults.

I'm all for forgiveness. It's important for our well-being and mental health. The difference is that Christians feel they need to believe in Christ to achieve forgiveness. When we do something that causes guilt, it's usually because of something we did to another person. It's the person we've wronged who we need to ask forgiveness from and not an abstract god. Forgiveness has to come from the heart and is not exclusive to people of faith.

If it's our fate to be judged by God, I believe everyone will be held accountable and judged the same way regardless of their religion. I find it difficult to comprehend that God would favor some people and reject others based on what they believe about him. We know we shouldn't judge others because of their religious beliefs. Why shouldn't we expect the same from God? It's just another example of where I think Christianity has it wrong.

*Religion as an addiction*

I've come to believe religion can be addictive. Addictions make it hard for people to control activities that bring them pleasure. This can be seen with drugs, tobacco, alcohol, sex, exercise, food, and shopping. Why not with religion? People return to pleasurable activities because the brain produces dopamine that creates a feeling of pleasure and well-being. Other reasons can be psychological. Some addictions are more harmful than others, but they all produce a loss of control over a pleasure-seeking activity. What I think drives most religious addictions is a need for unconditional love along with superstition. Those who are addicted to religion express their addiction by needing to spend a far greater amount of time than normal reading Scripture or devoting themselves to prayer. Another example of how this works with religion can be seen when people in church put themselves in a trancelike state during prayers and come out of it looking physically and emotionally spent. It gives meaning to the phrase getting high on Jesus. Religious addicts can sometimes act like drug addicts. They want others to enjoy the same "religious high" they experience and are quick to push their faith onto anyone who will listen. Most people don't exhibit that kind of extreme behavior when practicing their faith. That may be why some people see religion as playing a small part of their lives while others who are addicted immerse themselves in religion in a way that dominates and controls who they are. Some may even view the addiction to religion as a good thing while others will see it as just another out-of-control behavior.

Religions that make unusual or extreme demands on its members are labeled cults. It's not always easy to identify when a religion crosses that line.

Religion can also take the form of superstition. I've met a number of people who think if they stop attending church or stop believing that something bad will happen.

*Marketing religion*

It's interesting to look at how the marketing of Christianity has changed over time. In the Middle Ages, there was a greater emphasis placed on Satan, hell, and damnation. Over time, that message went out of favor. When it stopped working, the Christian movement had to adjust its message. Sometime ago, I read that talking about heaven was something ministers avoided since many people in their congregations couldn't imagine a better life than what they had on earth. Some churches have resorted to introducing rock music to attract the young. Today we have megachurches promoting the "feel good" message. They make the claim that all the worldly desires most people want in their lives such as love, happiness, and wealth can be theirs by accepting Christ. That movement's been coined the gospel of wealth. I find that message to be a contradiction to what I thought Jesus was about. In his Sermon on the Mount, Jesus said, *"It is easier for a camel to go through the eye of a needle than for a rich man to enter the kingdom of God"* (Matthew 19:24). He instructed his disciples to give everything away except the cloths on their backs. His words don't square with the emphasis many Christians place on acquiring wealth and material belongings through Christ.

Like any good marketing strategy, the message of Christianity changes to keep pace with what works. The selling of God is big business. Capturing souls in a highly competitive marketplace can reap financial rewards for the winners.

I could never understand how anyone (the clergy) could feel good about taking money from others for claiming to be certain about things no living being could possibly be certain about. It reminds me of the snake oil salesmen in the old west, who traveled the county selling bottles of a medical brew (mostly colored water) they claimed was a cure-all for everything that ails people. Strangely, some people claimed it cured them.

That brings me to the subject of televangelists. I've been watching them since I was a young boy. I watched them pray, heal the sick, and appeal to their viewers to send them money. They made fortunes talking about Jesus's love. Those who come to mind are Oral Roberts, Billy Graham, Jim and Tammy Baker, Pat Robertson, Benny Hinn, and Joel Osteen. In my opinion, they're frauds of the worst kind. They conned millions of innocent, mostly the elderly and poor, from their life savings in the name of Jesus. I could never understand why mainstream Christian church leaders remained silent about those kind of predatory practices. I can only conclude the brotherhood of Christianity, like the fraternal order of police, is blind when it comes to the failings of their own kind. One reason for their silence could be that all religious institutions rely on financial contributions and to attack others about their questionable claims and excess greed might cast a shadow on themselves.

*Tolerance*

The following statements come to mind when I think about religious tolerance because they remind me that all religions share many of the same characteristics:

> *Religions are different paths up the same mountain*

*My father's house has many mansions.*

*God is too big to fit inside just one religion.*

We need to keep in mind that most religions have more similarities than differences and should serve as a bond to bring people and nations together. The dialogue among people of different faiths should be based on mutual respect and trust rather than rejection and distrust. Sadly, I think organized religions have done more to polarize people than they have in uniting them. It would be nice if someday all the major religions could become the catalyst in helping us become just one human family. This would require a great deal less radicalism and more moderation than what I currently see among many religious leaders and their followers.

Intolerance comes when people confuse faith with facts. Religious beliefs are based on faith or hope that something is true. There's nothing wrong with faith so long as it's taken for what it is. We all have faith in something. It's when people begin to think faith beliefs are indisputable facts that religious fanaticism and extremism raises its ugly head.

The view of many religious radicals is that if everyone joined their faith, it would be a better world. That's particularly true for proselyting faiths like Muslims and Christians. Their goal is to convert the world. Some are so radical they would go to war to spread their faith. Most people know they'll never accomplish their goal, and until that kind of thinking is abandoned, we'll never be able to achieve world peace.

One way to reduce religious intolerance is to begin changing the way we raise our children. We put them in Bible school and other kinds of religious training in order to pass on our religious beliefs while intentionally or inadvertently passing along our prejudices and biases about people who believe differently or not at all. We could make it a better world if we included instruction about all the great religions in order for children to develop respect for people of all faiths or people who claim no religion. It would probably be a better world if we allowed them to grow up and discover their own beliefs instead of insisting they adopt ours. They might teach us more than we've been teaching them.

*Why doubt is not an option for religious leaders*

While writing this book and sharing my thoughts with people who play an active role in their religious institutions, I discovered many had no interest in wanting to hear facts or ideas that point out weaknesses in their faith. That puzzled me. I assumed everyone was interested in seeking the truth. I finally realized most religions have evolved into something like a living organism with a strong sense of survival. Acknowledging doubt threatens their existence. There are reasons for that.

One reason is power. Organized religions have always exerted power over their followers. To admit weakness might reduce that power, and that goes against their nature.

Another reason is that a great many people have a personal stake in defending their religious institutions. Many define themselves by their church affiliation. There are millions who make their livelihood ministering to others. Their economic well-being, self-worth, and social life are dependent on their church. Acknowledging weakness could represent a personal threat. Self-interest often has a higher priority than seeking the truth.

Ego is another consideration. When I watch some ministers give sermons, I sometimes think it's as much about them as it is about God. Saying to their congregation they're God's spokesmen and are all knowing when it comes to the truth about God can be intoxicating. Some even allow their followers to believe that through Christ, they have healing powers. That's not something they want to jeopardize by acknowledging doubt.

Religious institutions hold considerable wealth and are inherently wired to grow and gain economic strength in order to assure their survival. Any admitted weakness would weaken their appeal in the highly competitive religious marketplace. For many church leaders, when they found the Lord, they also found an unending source of wealth in the form of tax-free contributions from their followers. Financial well-being often takes precedence over truth.

All those observations may seem overly simplistic, but I believe they hold some degree of truth and help explain why so many church leaders and their followers are so protective and defensive when their beliefs are being challenged. It also helps explain why there is so little acceptance and open dialogue among leaders of different religions. Power, self-interest, ego, social status, and financial well-being can't be ignored even in the religious community.

*Letter to grandchildren*

To help give the reader some insight into what I believe, I'll share a letter I wrote to my grandchildren to give to them during their teenage years. We have two sons and ten grandchildren. I wrote this letter in 1999 when I was fifty-eight years old.

I prefaced it with this: *"As a young man, I always thought it would have been nice if an older person would have shared with me what they learned about life. That never happened so I'm sharing what I learned with you."*

## What I Learned

*Always try to do what's right. This may sound easy but it's one of life's greatest challenges. To fail is to have regrets. When in doubt listen to your conscience.*

*Be honest with yourself and others and take responsibility for your actions.*

*Try not to be judgmental. Learn tolerance and remember all behavior is caused. That said, I admit to being critical of people and institutions that are intolerant and judgmental.*

*Help others when you can, especially those who are in need.*

*Take responsibility for your own happiness. I once heard the definition of happiness is having someone to love, something to do and something to look forward to.*

*We all carry unwanted baggage in life. Learn to live with it and use it to your advantage. Don't let it be an excuse for failure.*

*Choose a career based on what you enjoy doing but be realistic. Most importantly develop a good work ethic. Without it life will always be a struggle.*

*Don't become too preoccupied with acquiring material things. I've found the greatest pleasures in life are free.*

*Choose your marriage partner well. It's the most important decision you'll make. I did this well when I married your grandmother, as did your parents. One test in choosing a partner is to look at your future partner's parents and ask if you'd be happy being a spouse in that relationship. For good or bad most of us become like our parents in many ways.*

*Work hard and be loyal to your employer. When you can't be loyal it's time to move on.*

*Money isn't the most important thing in life but without it life can be difficult. There's nothing inherently wrong with acquiring wealth. Learn how to save and invest. Financial independence can provide you with freedom of choice, comfort, security and the ability to help others.*

*Learn to live a balanced life: work, family and play. I wasn't good at that.*

*Don't use controlled substances. I made the mistake of smoking. Alcohol is okay unless it becomes a problem. Then quit.*

*Religion can be a good thing but like everything else in life it's best when practiced in moderation. Learn to distinguish between faith and facts. Don't fall victim to letting others think for you. Be open to all the possibilities. There's much to be learned.*

*Respect all life and protect the environment. (The Right to Life and a woman's right to choose is a separate issue from this and one that reasonable people can disagree about with neither side being entirely right or wrong).*

*The older you get the more you'll find there are few absolutes in life. Be a life time learner.*

*The best thing that can be said about our journey through life is that we tried to leave the world a better place than we found it. It doesn't have to be in a world altering way but in the little things that matter. One measure is that we gave more than we took.*

*Respect your parents.*
*This one is probably the most important. Be sure to always wear clean underwear in case you're*

*in an accident. Grandma really likes this one. It's
been in her family a long time.*

*Love,*
*Grandma & Grandpa*

This was a challenging exercise and was not as easy as it appears. I would urge everyone over fifty to give it a try.

# In Closing

Some people may think I'm going to hell for my views about God and religion. They'd probably find it hard to believe that I hold the opposite view. I have faith that if there is a God, he'll thank me for trying to set the record straight. I think he'll agree with me that he's been poorly served by people and their religions throughout history. I know he won't fault me for attempting to seek the truth. If there is no god, my message is even more important. Whatever the outcome, I'm more than willing to take my chances.

I want to thank those of you who have taken the time to read my journey in search of truth. I hope it was a good read for you and you weren't offended. It was not my intention. I hope my book was thought-provoking and interesting.

# Recommended Reading

Barker, Dan. *Losing Faith in Faith.* Madison, Wisconsin: Freedom from Religion Foundation Inc., 2003.

Dawkins, Richard. *The God Delusion.* New York, New York: Houghton Mifflin Company, 2006.

Ehrman, Bart D. *Revealing the Hidden Contradictions in the Bible (and Why We Don't Know About Them).* New York, New York: HarperCollins, 2009.

Harris, Sam. *Letter to a Christian Nation.* New York, New York: Alfred A. Knopf, 2006.

Holmes, David L. *The Faiths of the Founding Fathers.* Oxford, New York: Oxford University Press, 2006.

Meacham, Jon. *American Gospel.* New York, New York: Random House Inc., 2006.

Tabor, James D. *The Jesus Dynasty.* New York, New York: Simon & Schuster, 2006.

# Source Notes

*The Search*

Barker, 368. He says nothing about miracles; fixes no historical times or places to events surrounding the life of Jesus; makes no references to the twelve apostles by name; omits the trial and doesn't name the location and place of the crucifixion.

Brunner, Borgna. 2004. *TIME Almanac 2005*. 160 Gould Street, Needham, MA. 358. People who don't subscribe to any religion are the fastest growing group in the United States.

*"How Many People Go Regularly to Weekly Religious Services."* 2005. ReligiousTolerance.Org. Ontario Consultants on Religious Tolerance, n.d. http://www.religioustolerance.org/rel_rate.htm. Most pollsters agree that between 70 and 80 percent of the people in the US don't attend church on a regular basis, and that even though the vast majority claim to believe in God, close to a third don't believe in the biblical God.

*Christ and Christianity*

2004. *"Religions of the World: Numbers of Adherents; names of houses of worship, names of leaders, rates of growth…" n.d.* http://www. religioustolerance.org/rel_rate.htm. About 34,000 different Christian denominations throughout the world.

2004. *"The Rule of St. Augustine,"* n.d. http://www.geocities.com/ Athens/1534/ruleaug.html#Moderation%20and%20Self%20 Denial.

Barker, Dan. 2006. *Losing Faith in Faith.* Freedom from Religion Foundation Inc. PO Box 750, Madison, WI. 361–364.

However, most scholars believe the references to Jesus that Christians refer to were forged and added sometimes during the beginning of the fourth century.

Barker. p. 368. Paul doesn't recount any of the miracles.

Bowen, Jeremy, et. al. 2001. "Jesus the Complete Story," BBC video. Aired on the Discovery Channel. Forensic medical artists have recently used modern scientific methods to recreate his appearance based on what people looked like during his time in that region. That would be short, dark hair, dark eyes dark complexion; prominent nose and a broad face. He looked like many of the Arabs living in the region today.

Dawkins, Richard. 2006. *The God Delusion.* Houghton Mifflin Company, Boston & New York. 95. "Matthew traces Joseph's descent from King David via twenty-eight intermediate generations, while Luke has forty-one generations." To make matters worse, there is almost no overlap in the names on the two lists.

Ibid. 157. They (John and Jesus) believed they were living in the "last days" or the "end of the age."

Ibid. 154–155. "God would raise up a King of the line of David who would be instrumental in throwing off foreign rule and establishing an independent Kingdom of Israel, thus inaugurating the New Age of peace and justice in the entire world."

Ibid. 172. "The good news of the Kingdom of God predicted the apocalyptic reversal of society from top to bottom. Those in power would fall, and those oppressed would be lifted."

Ibid. 280. Contrary to popular belief, they anticipated a kingdom on earth and not in heaven.

Ibid. 244. James, the brother of Jesus, became the successor of Jesus and the undisputed leader of the Christian movement after his death.

Ibid. 261. Paul was a Roman citizen who saw himself as the "Apostle to the Gentiles," viewing himself as the thirteenth apostle.

Ibid. 267. He de-emphasized the Jewishness of Jesus insisting Gentile converts were not required to be circumcised or live as Jews under the Torah.

Ehrman, Bart D. 2010. *Jesus, Interrupted.* HarperCollins, New York, NY. 103. Most scholars now believe Jesus's followers couldn't read or write and couldn't have been authors of the Gospels. It's believed they were written anonymously with none of the writers being an eyewitness to the events they wrote about.

Ibid. 106. Most believe they were written by highly educated, Greek-speaking Christians who probably lived somewhere outside of Palestine.

Ibid. 149. The first documented historical record of anything written about him was in AD 112.

Ibid. 220–221. Contrary to popular belief, the twenty-seven books of the New Testament were never officially approved by a church council. They evolved over a three hundred-year period driven by numerous historical and cultural factors within the Christian movement. They were first put forth by Athanasius, the bishop of Alexandria, Egypt in AD 367 and later became the de facto list that Christians have come to know as the New Testament.

Ehrman. 245–249. Three of the gospels writers don't call Jesus God. In none of the speeches in Acts is Jesus spoken as divine. For ancient Jews, being "the Son of God" didn't mean divine. In the Old Testament, it meant being the human intermediary for God on earth or the one God has chosen to do his will. John, who was an advocate for Paul, is the only gospel that identifies Jesus divine.

Ibid. 94. John links Christ with God at the very birth of the universe. Mark claims it happened with his baptism. Matthew and Luke identify Christ with becoming the Son of God with the Nativity and Paul on the day of his resurrection.

Ehrman. 40. Mark, Matthew, and Luke say it lasted a few months and John says three years.

Ehrman. 84. "John claims he performed them to convince people to believe in him."

Ibid. 84. "Matthew claims he didn't perform miracles to prove himself but only to help those in need."

Liston, Broward/Orlando, Amanda Bower/New York, Helen Gibson/London, and Marguerite Michaels/Arlington Heights. *Behind the First Noel. Time, December 13, 2004.* 53 and 58. The use of stars marking historical events were common in those days. Stars were associated with the founding of Rome and the fall of Jerusalem, along with the birth of Alexander the Great and Augustus Caesar.

Ibid. *53. 51–52.* Matthew and Luke's version of the birth of Christ. A census did take place twelve years later.

Liston, Bower, Gibson, Michaels. 54. An immaculate conception was not an unusual belief during Jesus's times. Non-Jews believed in divine conception in stories about Plato, Alexander the Great, and Augustus Caesar. It also appeared in Greek and Roman mythology.

Tabor, James D. 2006. *The Jesus Dynasty. The Hidden History of Jesus, His Royal Family, and the Birth of Christianity.* New York, NY; Simon & Schuster. 282. Jesus believed he was the Davidic Messiah.

Ibid. 280. Made no claim of being the Son of God. He attributes Paul, who never met Jesus but claims to have seen him in a vision for planting that seed.

Tabor. 135. In Tabor's quest for the historical Jesus, he believes it was John the baptizer (Jesus's cousin) who first preached about the kingdom of God, and it was Jesus who joined him and his movement thus becoming a disciple of John.

Tabor. 273. "Christ as the divine, preexistent Son of God who took on human form, died on the cross for the sins of the world, and was resurrected to heavenly glory at God's right hand…"

Ibid. 264. It was Paul who declared Jesus's purpose was to die on the cross as atonement for the sins of the world and that those who accept his atoning sacrifice will receive the gift of eternal life.

Ibid. 249. He's named as the author of thirteen of the twenty-seven books of the New Testament. The book of Acts (written by Luke) is almost entirely a defense of Paul's revelations as the thirteenth apostle. Luke was a pro-Roman, a Gentile, and the only non-Jewish writer in the New Testament.

Tabor. 274. "James directly disputed Paul's teaching of salvation by faith without the deeds of the law."

Tabor. 235. The Jewish tradition required that a corpse must be buried within twenty-four hours after the death. Since Jesus's body had been rushed to a temporary tomb because of the Passover holiday, it makes sense that the family would want to complete his burial as soon as possible. That would have included washing and anointing his body.

Ibid. 231. Tabor claims the story first appeared in a letter written by Paul to the 1 Corinthians in AD 54.

Ibid. 230. The original version of the gospel of Mark says nothing about his resurrection and appearances after his death. His account ends with the empty tomb.

Ibid. 231. Scribes who copied Mark made up the ending that appears in Mark some three hundred years after the original text was composed.

Ibid. 228–229. The versions of that event from John, Matthew, and Luke's are different. "They don't agree as to who arrived first at the tomb and what subsequently transpired…"

Tabor. 44. There are also claims that after learning she was pregnant, Mary left town to stay with close family relatives (Elizabeth and Zechariah the parents of John the baptizer who lived in Ein Kerem).

Ibid., 59–63. There are references in early writings about Jesus that suggests he was "born of fornication and not divine intervention."

*"The Unknown Jesus,"* Biography Special for A&E Network. Produced by Filmroose Inc. 1999. Jesus's link with Buddhism.

"The Unknown Jesus," strong probability he was married and the reasons.

Underwood, Anne. 1999. "2000 Years of Jesus." *Newsweek.* 52. The quote, "Historians did not record his birth…"


*Observations and Myth Busting*


Adler, Jerry. 2007. "A Big Dose of Skepticism." *Newsweek. 22.* Studies show that it's not unusual for a third of the patients in clinical trials who take placebos and not the drug being tested to get better. This is particularly true with conditions such as pain or depression.

Benson, H., et al. 2006. "Study of the therapeutic effects of intercessory prayer (STEP) in cardiac bypass patients." *American Heart Journal*. 934–42. It found no difference between those patients who were prayed for and those who were not. In fact, those who were prayed for, and knew it, did a little worse.

Cheng, Marcia. 2007. http://www.newsvine.com/_news/2007/10/11/1019458legalstatusdoesntdeterabortion. Studies show women are just as likely to get an abortion in countries where it's legal as they are in countries where it's outlawed…

Holmes, David L. 2006. *The Faiths of the Founding Fathers*. Oxford University Press, Oxford New York. 50–51. That would include Franklin, Washington, Jefferson, Madison, and Monroe.

Harris, Sam. 2006. *Letter to a Christian Nation*. Alfred A. Knopf, a division of Random House Inc. 16. There is no place in the New Testament where Jesus denounces the practice.

Harris. *38*. Fifty percent of all human conceptions end up in a spontaneous abortion with woman often not even knowing they were pregnant. Twenty percent of all recognized pregnancies end up in miscarriages. It could be argued God is the most prolific of the abortionists.

Goodstein, Laurie. 2004. "*Two Studies Cite Child Sex Abuse by 4% of Priests,*" n.d. National Desk, Late Edition. http://select.nytimes.com/gst/abstract.html?res=FB0813FC3A580C748ED-DAB0894DC404482&n=Top%2fReference%2fTimes%20Topics%2fOrganizations%2fJ%2fJohn%20Jay%20College%20of%20Criminal%20Justice. Final Section A, Page 1, column 1. Sexual molestation of children within the Catholic church.

*A Source of Unity and Peace or Division and Conflict*

"*Anti-Semitism and Anti-Judaism within the Roman Catholic Church First to Twentieth Century ce,*" n.d. 2004. http://www.religioustolerance.org/vat_hol11.htm. Jews being blamed for Jesus's death.

*An Overview of 2000 Years of Jewish Persecution Anti-Judaism: 1201 1800 CE,"* n.d. *Ontario Consultants on Religious Tolerance,* n.d. 2005. http://www.religioustolerance.org/jud_pers3.htm. Jewish persecution of Jews. This site contains a more comprehensive list of Jewish persecution than contained in this book.

Ibid., (Anti-Semitism: Racially based persecution of Jews 1800 to 1946). Jewish persecution of Jews. This site contains a more comprehensive list of Jewish persecution than contained in this book.

Dawkins. 273–274. Hitler was raised a Catholic and attended Catholic schools. There's no evidence he ever renounced his faith.

Harris. 12. Martin Luther and John Calvin, the two Protestant founders, advocated the wholesale murder of heretics, apostates, Jews, and witches.

*"Religions of the World: Numbers of Adherents; names of houses of worship, names of leaders, rates of growth..."* n.d. 2004. http://www. religioustolerance.org/rel_rate.htm. Religious Breakdown by Population (2000).


*What It All Means*


Barker. 333. "He drowned the entire population of the planet, saving one family. He sent the plague to kill all first born children in Egypt, human and animal. He rained fire and brimstone on Sodom, killing everyone—boys, girls, babies, pregnant women, animals. He sent his Israelite warriors to destroy the neighboring pagan tribes, man, woman, and children."

# *About the Author*

Alex Vercellino is a retired educator. His book about Christianity and his search for truth took more than a decade of research, writing, soliciting input and numerous rewrites. He's no stranger to faith and mortality having worked at a funeral home while in college and volunteering at a cancer treatment center and Hospice in Key West, Florida during his retirement years. He's a survivor of stage three lung cancer and metastatic brain cancer. He currently resides in Walled Lake, Michigan. Alex lost his wife from dementia after sixty-one years of marriage. They have two sons, ten grandchildren and ten great-grandchildren.